3 9066 00549313 1

W9-CIZ-637

BOOKSALE

MAY 2 2 1990

GREATER VICTORIA
PUBLIC LIBRARY

S. V. BRANCH

WORDS
CAN TELL
. . .

309946

WORDS
CAN TELL
• • •

A Book About
Our Language

CHRISTINA ASHTON

JULIAN MESSNER

S. V. BRANCH

GREATER VICTORIA PUBLIC LIBRARY

• • •

Text copyright © 1988 by Christina Ashton
Illustrations copyright © 1988 by Janie Paul
All rights reserved including the right of reproduction in whole or in part in any form. Published by Julian Messner, a division of Silver Burdett Press, Inc., Simon & Schuster, Inc., Prentice Hall Bldg., Englewood Cliffs, NJ 07632.

JULIAN MESSNER and colophon are trademarks of Simon & Schuster, Inc.
Manufactured in the United States of America.
          10 9 8 7 6 5 4 3 2 1

**Library of Congress
Cataloging-in-Publication Data**

Ashton, Christina.
   Words can tell.

   Includes index.
   Summary: An introduction to the history of the English language, from ancient times to the present day, including the histories of a selection of words in everyday use.
   1. English language—History—Juvenile literature.   2. English language—Etymology—Juvenile literature. [1. English language—History.   2. English language—Etymology]   I. Title.
PE125.A84   1988   422
87-20333
ISBN 0-617-65223-0
                    • • •

The first part of this book tells about how English came to be the language it is today and the different ways words continue to come into our language. Most of our words are the result of a long, slow process of change, or evolution, from older languages. But not all of our words can be traced back in time. Many were simply invented at different times over the centuries. As a matter of fact, we continue to invent words every day. When we are not inventing new words, we are borrowing them from other languages. And, finally, many of our words were originally the names of people and places.

The second part of the book tells the stories behind some words in each category. There are stories behind old words like *ballot* and *gossip;* behind invented words like *bazooka* and *hobby;* behind borrowed words like *coconut, dumbbell, robe;* and behind people and place names like *canter, lynch* and *sandwich.* The word stories try to go further than the dictionary does to explain a word.

C O N T E N T S

INTRODUCTION 1

───────── ·PART·ONE· ─────────
WHERE OUR WORDS COME FROM

1·PEOPLE LEARN TO TALK 5
2·THE ANCESTOR LANGUAGES 7
3·LANGUAGE FAMILIES GROW AND
   BRANCH OUT 12
4·BEFORE OLD ENGLISH 16
5·OLD ENGLISH 22
6·MIDDLE ENGLISH 27
7·MODERN ENGLISH 34
8·BORROWED WORDS 41
9·NORTH AMERICAN INDIAN
   WORDS 49
10·INVENTED AND OTHER
   WORDS 52

·PART·TWO·
WORD STORIES

11 · BORROWED WORDS   61
    Assassin/Assassination   61
    Barbecue/Buccaneer   62
    Coconut   65
    Dumbbell   66
    Easel   67
    Filibuster   68
    Marathon   70
    Marmalade   72
    Robe   73
    Sabotage   74
    Thug   75

12 · INVENTED WORDS   77
    Bangs   77
    Bazooka   78
    Hobby/Hobby Horse   79
    Phony   81

13 · PEOPLE AND PLACE NAMES   83
    Bedlam   83
    Canter   85
    Chauvinist   86
    Guy   87
    Lynch   89
    Sandwich   90
    Sequoia   92
    Spoonerism   95

14 · OLD WORDS   96
    Abacus/Calculate/Calculator/
    Calculus   96
    Applaud/Explode   97
    Ballot/Blackball   99

Berserk   100
Blackmail   102
Bonfire   103
Chess/Checkmate/Exchequer/
Checkers/Check   105
Curfew   108
Debonair   109
Dismal   110
Dragon/Dragoon   112
Fanatic   113
Gossip   115
Handicap   117
Idiot   118
Infantry   119
Kidnap   121
Money   122
Pen/Pencil/Penicillin   126
Salary   127
Sirloin   128
Slave/Slav   129
Sleuth   129
Tawdry   131
Town/Metropolis/City/Village/
Hamlet   132
Urchin   134
Yankee   134
Gringo   136

INDEX   137

For Jerry, who never let me give up

WORDS
CAN TELL
. . .

INTRODUCTION
• • •

In this book we will make a brief search for the roots of our language. The search will tell us something about the words we use every day. Knowing something about our words will help us to find out something about ourselves and our ancestors.

Words are like little crystal balls. If you stare long and deeply enough into them, words can show you all the funny, horrible, joyous, brave, sorrowful and wondrous things people have done since they first began to talk, long ago, in the shadowy time known as prehistory.

Words can tell us when, where, how and why people have worked and played, made war and made peace, invented and destroyed. Words can tell us which people were sinners and which were saints, which were geniuses and which were fools, and which were all the different kinds of ordinary people in between. The study of words is really the study of human kind.

For a simple study of a word there is always the dictionary. A dictionary tells you how a word is spelled and pronounced, what it means, how it is used and where it came from.

This book tells more about where words come from. The dictionary is very brief on a word's history and tells us about it in mysterious abbreviations that are hard to understand. For example, look up the word *check*. You will see that there are many meanings for that word. Meaning number one, the dictionary tells us, comes from:

"ME *chek* fr. OF *eschec* fr. Ar *shah* fr. Pers. lit. *king* akin to Gk. *ktasthai to acquire*."

What all these abbreviations mean is this: *Check* comes from the Middle English word *chek*. *Chek* comes from the Old French word *eschec*. *Eschec* comes from the Arabic word *shah*. *Shah* comes from a Persian word which literally means "king," and which is related to the Greek word *ktasthai*, which means "to acquire." But all of this is only part of the story.

The rest of the story is in this book, which takes up where the dictionary leaves off. It tells the who, what, when, where and why of the word between, for example, "ME *chek*" and "Pers. *shah*." You will be surprised at the source and original meaning of such common, everyday words as *bangs, bonfire, guy, canter* and *thug*. If you like riddles, think about these: What does sabotage have to do with shoes? What does salt have to do with money? Can what people did, and when, where and why they did it explain why our words are what they are today?

PART
ONE

WHERE OUR
WORDS
COME FROM

1

PEOPLE LEARN TO TALK
. . .

No one knows exactly when humans first began to form words. There is the "bow-wow" theory of language which says that the first words were imitations of the sounds of nature. According to this theory, early language might have been a series of sounds which took on the meaning of the things they imitated. "Boom" might have meant thunder, for example, or "chirp" could have meant bird. "Bow-wow" could have meant dog, and still does, in the baby talk of many languages.

The dictionary calls words like boom and chirp imitative words, and modern English has many of them. Listen to the sounds and think of the meanings of giggle, splash or burp. Many birds and insects are named for the sounds they make. If you have ever heard the cry of a cuckoo or the chirp of a cricket it is easy to see why they have the names they have.

In other languages besides English, words often imitate sounds. In Spanish cricket is *grillo* (GREE-yo). Splash in Spanish is *chapotear* (chop-o-tay-ARE). That word definitely has the sound of a belly flop off a high diving board.

But the bow-wow theory does not explain how or when people formed the words for ideas and feelings, such as love, hate, peace, anger, belief, enemy, friend. Nor does it explain about the source of prepositions and adverbs that express time and place—words such as before, after, in, out, near, far, and so on. There is much disagreement about how language began. We may never know for certain, simply because we cannot go back in time to hear the first words spoken. It was only when writing was invented that we could learn more about the words of our ancestors, and how those words came to be the words we use today.

Just exactly who was the first person to write and exactly when it was done are as mysterious as the beginnings of speech. But we can guess that somewhere along the line people saw the need for a more permanent form of communication than speech. Spoken words are easily forgotten. Written words can be referred to again and again. Since we have so few facts about this early time we can only imagine when and how people thought up symbols and began marking them down. It is possible someone began by making scratches on a piece of bark, because the earliest word we know for write is *writan,* which means "to scratch," and our word book comes from *boc,* the name of the bark of the beech tree.

Writing is a set of symbols which stand for objects, ideas and the sounds of speech. The story of the development of writing and of the alphabets of the world is another book in itself. We mention it here to show how language scholars, or linguists, discovered the very early beginnings of the English we speak today.

The most important discovery linguists made about language is that words, like people, come in families. Languages do not just suddenly spring up all by themselves out of nowhere; they are related to each other, and take a long time to develop. Linguists reasoned that if languages are related to each other, then many of them must have come from a single ancestor thousands of years ago. English, they found, is a cousin of most of the languages spoken in the western world today.

2

THE ANCESTOR LANGUAGES
• • •

About three hundred years ago, scholars noticed similarities in languages which were very different from each other. Some Greek words, for example, were found to be almost the same in spelling and meaning as some German words. But the scholars had not been able to determine why these words were similar. Then, about two hundred years ago, centuries after these languages began, linguists discovered an ancient written language called Sanskrit, from the region of East India. Sanskrit is known as a dead language because it has not been spoken for thousands of years.

By comparing the Sanskrit alphabet with other ancient and modern alphabets, scholars could see similarities in symbols and the sounds for which the symbols stood. From these similarities they reasoned that languages as vastly different as Irish, Persian and Dutch—not to mention French, English and German—all seemed to come from one original tongue, or "ancestor" language. This ancestor language is now called Indo-European. It was not a written language, but because of the discovery of Sanskrit, which forms a link between modern written languages

7

and ancient Indo-European, scholars can guess at what it was probably like. Experts believe that most of the languages spoken today in the Americas, Britain, Europe, the Middle East and parts of India come from Indo-European.

How do we know that all these languages come from Indo-European? How do we know this theory is true? What evidence do we have? The most interesting piece of evidence which proves that this theory is probably true is this: Modern Lithuanians, who live in northeastern Europe along the Baltic Sea, can read and understand a few words in Sanskrit. This is astonishing, first because Sanskrit was a language of East India, many hundreds of miles away from Lithuania; and second because Sanskrit has not even been *spoken* for thousands of years! Here, then, was proof that the Lithuanian and Sanskrit languages were related.

If all these languages have a single ancestor, how did they become so different? Why can't an Irishman converse with a Greek, or a Frenchman with a Lithuanian, or a North American with a Spaniard? The answer to this, the experts tell us, is that the ancient Indo-Europeans moved far and wide from each other and settled in new places. From their homeland somewhere in central Europe, they moved east as far as India, west as far as the British Isles, and as far south as the north coast of Africa. As they settled in places that were different from their old homes they developed new customs and ways of life more suitable to their new surroundings. Life in a land by the sea would be very different from life in a land of forests and rivers, and mountain people lived differently from people in valleys. As a result of all this movement and change, languages had to grow and change to fit new conditions. New words were needed, and old words, if they were not needed, were forgotten.

Some of the branches of Indo-European are classified into groups called Indo-Iranian, Balto-Slavic, Hellenic (Greek), Celtic, Italic and Germanic. Each of these groups is broken down into other groups of languages, some of which died out com-

INDO-EUROPEAN LANGUAGES

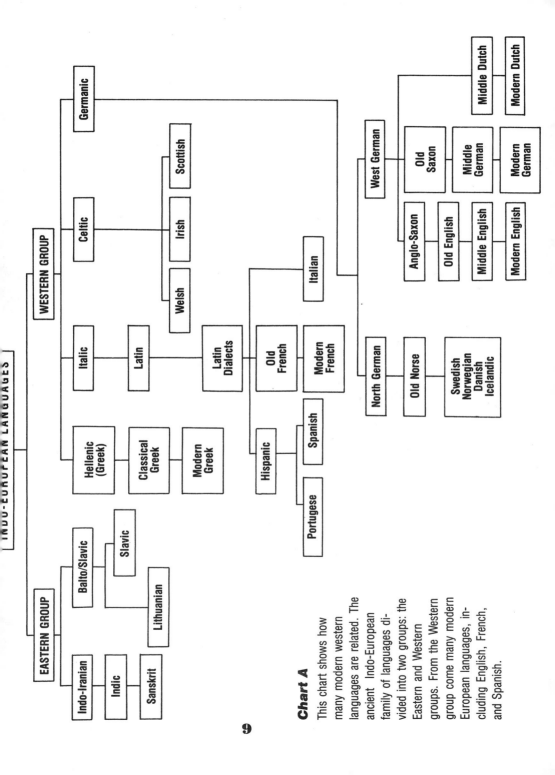

Chart A

This chart shows how many modern western languages are related. The ancient Indo-European family of languages divided into two groups: the Eastern and Western groups. From the Western group come many modern European languages, including English, French, and Spanish.

9

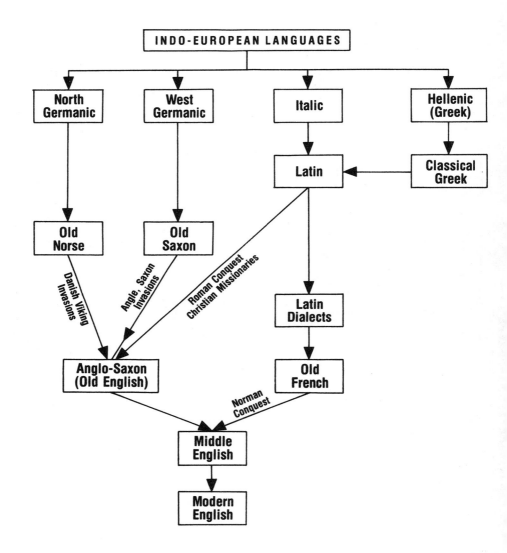

INDO-EUROPEAN LANGUAGES

North Germanic → West Germanic → Italic → Hellenic (Greek)

Italic → Latin ← Classical Greek (Hellenic)

North Germanic → Old Norse

West Germanic → Old Saxon

Old Norse → *Danish Viking Invasions* → Anglo-Saxon (Old English)

Old Saxon → *Anglo-Saxon Invasions* → Anglo-Saxon (Old English)

Latin → *Roman Conquest Christian Missionaries* → Anglo-Saxon (Old English)

Latin → Latin Dialects → Old French

Anglo-Saxon (Old English) → Middle English

Old French → *Norman Conquest* → Middle English

Middle English → Modern English

Chart B

This chart shows how different languages contributed to the development of English. Roman soldiers and later Christian missionaries brought Latin to England, and invaders from northern Europe brought old Norse and Saxon languages. Later still, the Norman Conquest brought the Old English language into contact with Old French.

pletely, and some of which continued to change, or evolve, into modern languages.

Of the Italic languages, Latin is one of the most ancient. Latin remained a spoken language clear into the twentieth century in the religious ceremonies of the Catholic Church. It remains alive as a written language, and some of the oldest and newest words in English come from Latin. Italian, Spanish, Portuguese, French and Roumanian, known as the Romance languages, are all later forms, or dialects, of Latin. Of these Romance languages, French has the greatest influence on English.

The Germanic languages are the nearest relatives to English. Other Germanic languages are Icelandic, Norwegian, Danish, Swedish, Dutch and German. The charts on pages 9 and 10 show how these groups developed from the original into the languages of today. Chart A shows the relationships of most of the Indo-European languages to each other. Chart B shows those languages that had the most important influence on English.

3

LANGUAGE FAMILIES GROW AND BRANCH OUT
...

It is hard to believe that so many widely different languages can be related to each other and have a common ancestor. But both the differences and similarities among them can be explained by the constant movement of peoples for thousands of years. Eventually there were so many different pronunciations of any one word that only the most careful scholar could trace that word back to its common ancestor.

But careful scholars have found that some everyday little words have hardly changed at all from what they guess to be the original Indo-European. For example, pronouns—words such as "you" or "I" that tell us who we are—seem to be closely related to Indo-European when we see them written, although they sound quite different from each other when we hear them pronounced.

I in modern English comes from an earlier form of our language called Old English. In that language it was *ic.* In modern German I is *ich;* in Dutch, *ik;* in Italian, *io* and in Spanish, *yo.* The Indo-European word was *eg.* This might be hard to connect with the modern forms, but think of the word ego, which is Latin for the pronoun "I" and in modern English is the word for "self."

In Indo-European the words for me and we were exactly the same as they are today in English. You was *yu*.

The very important little words is and be come directly from Indo-European, and you can see the similarities of those words in many different languages. The English "is" is *ist* in German, *es* in Spanish and *est* in French. These forms come from the Latin *esse*. The Indo-European ancestor word was *es*. *Bheu* is the Indo-European ancestor for be.

Here are three common everyday words: mother, night, and seven. Look at the columns below to see how similar these words are in languages as different from one another as modern Dutch and ancient Sanskrit.

Mother		*Night*		*Seven*	
Dutch	moeder	German	nocht	German	sieben
Icelandic	mðir*	Dutch	nacht	Dutch	zeven
Danish	moder	Swedish	nott	Swedish	sju
Irish	mathir	Latin	noctis	Latin	septem
Russian	mate	French	nuit	French	sept
Lithuanian	mote	Spanish	noche	Spanish	siete
Latin	mater	Italian	notte	Italian	sette
Persian	madar	Roumanian	noapte	Roumanian	sapte
Sanskrit	matr	Greek	nuktos	Greek	hepta
		Polish	noc	Polish	siedem
* has a *th* sound		Czech	noc	Czech	sedm
		Russian	noch	Russian	syem
		Sanskrit	nakta	Sanskrit	sapta

Notice that seven in Greek is *hepta*. This is so different from the other words for seven that we might think it came from a completely different ancestor language. But linguists discovered that some time during the centuries of the Indo-

Europeans migrations to the west, east and south, there was a regular pattern of pronunciation changes. Once they understood this pattern and could see it was regular, scholars could trace even the most dissimilar words back to their origin in a common source.

We do not need to go into the details of these complicated changes. It is enough to know that after years of painstaking work, linguists have discovered that words come in families. There are many, many word families, and some families have many branches. Words as different from one another as water, whiskey, vodka, winter, sound and hydrant are all of the same family and have a common ancestor, the Indo-European *awer,* which means "wet" or "to flow." The same is true of rajah, royal, surge, regular, rectangle and correct. These come from the Indo-European *reg* which meant both "straight" and "king." Tree is of the same family as true, tar and tray, coming from the Indo-European *dru* which meant "tree."

By far the majority of English words are the result of hundreds of years of evolution from old, old words which came from the languages of most of the western world. So, when we study the history of English we really study a great deal of the history of Europe and the Middle East. We have seen that some of the mysterious differences and similarities among languages can be explained by the constant movement of peoples. Throughout the history of the world, groups of people have moved away from each other to build new societies. Generations later, they have come back into contact with each other through trade and warfare. In Europe and the Middle East, over the past fifteen hundred years, certain of these events were very important to the development of the English we speak today. If these events had not occurred, or if the results had been different, today we might very well be speaking not English, but French, Arabic, Persian, Danish, or even Mongolian Chinese. It is even possible that we would be speaking a language entirely different from any of these, a language we can only imagine. But the events did take place, and in order to understand why our language is made up of words like bedlam, check, dime, explode, gossip, idiot, kidnap, lynch, money, pen, slave, and yankee, we have to take a quick look at history between the first century A.D. and the present.

4

BEFORE OLD ENGLISH

The English language we speak today went through three stages called Old English, Middle English and Modern English. But ages before even Old English came into being, many other languages had to arise and develop. The oldest of these, as far as we know, was the Indo-European family of languages, which were beginning to be spoken clear back during the Stone Age. During the Stone Age, some Indo-European people lived on the islands of Britain.

The earliest known of these British Indo-Europeans split into two groups called the Scots and the Celts. There was another group, who were not Indo-European, called Picts. Together these three peoples are known as Britons. The Britons were a fierce, Stone Age people constantly making war on each other. They dressed in animal skins, lived in caves or rude wooden huts and had a religion which included human sacrifice. The fiercest of them all were the Picts, who painted their faces blue and scared their enemies to death as often as they slaughtered them with wooden clubs. The Picts and Scots lived in the northern and western parts of Britain, and the Celts in the east and south and in Ireland. These people had their own languages. The Celts were probably the first of them to come into contact with people from other parts of the world and to be influenced by new, foreign languages. As the languages of the Britons developed, it would come into contact with new, foreign languages again and again over the centuries, as we will see.

At the same time that the Stone Age Britons were living their warlike life, the Greeks, far to the east of them, were building a great civilization in Europe. Many of our ideas of art, literature, science, philosophy and government today come from the genius of these ancient people. As the Greek civilization reached a high point, another great civilization was being built in Italy by the Romans, whose language was Latin. When the Romans conquered Greece and made it part of their empire, they found a culture much older and far superior to their own. So they borrowed it. Roman art, sculpture, architecture, religion, medicine and science were actually basically Greek. The Greek language had much influence on Latin.

In a thousand years, the Roman Empire grew to include all of southern and central Europe and parts of the Middle East, including what is now Egypt, Israel, Syria, Lebanon and Turkey. It was the largest empire the world had ever known, and as the empire grew, the influence of the Latin language spread.

After conquering all of Europe, Rome invaded Britain and made it part of the empire, in A.D. 43. Romans brought their advanced culture to the Britons. Not only did they bring their art, literature, law and the Latin language, they established schools, built buildings and roads and provided an army to protect themselves against invaders. It was the southern Celts, a more peaceful people than the Picts and Scots, who were conquered by the Romans. The Picts and Scots were so fierce that even the excellent Roman armies could not defeat them. They did, however, manage to push these Britons north and keep them there by building a wall. You can see the ruins of that wall today. It is called Hadrian's Wall, after the Roman emperor who ordered it built.

The Celts enjoyed the peace and protection provided by Rome for about four hundred years. During that time, Celtic continued to be the language of the people, but Roman schools taught reading and writing to a small number of people. The few writings that were set down in Celtic were in the Roman alphabet, which is very like the alphabet we use today.

Meanwhile, the Germanic peoples of northern Europe were developing another, separate European culture. They did not build cities, investigate science or create much art or literature as did the Greeks and Romans. They were wandering tribes of hunters, sailors and warriors, as fierce as the Britons.

The Germanic people split into many different groups, but all together they are known as "Norsemen" or "Northmen." An early group of Norsemen, called Lombards, moved into northern Italy. Another group, the Franks, settled into what is now France. Franks and Lombards began as warlike, uncivilized people, but those who moved south from their homelands settled down and began to live in peace. Their descendants stopped wandering and became farmers. As the Roman Empire grew, it first took over the Lombards and then the Franks. This explains why the French language became a combination of Latin and a Germanic language called Frankish.

Other groups of Norsemen came to be known as Angles, Saxons, Jutes and Goths. They moved into what is now Denmark, Norway, Sweden, Holland and parts of Germany. They were warriors, but also sailors and traders. In very early times the Angles and Saxons began to trade with the Celts in England. This was probably the first time the Britons came into contact with other peoples.

Although Rome had built a mighty empire which easily took over early Germanic peoples such as the Lombards and the Franks, it was never able to push far enough into northern Europe to defeat the Germanic people who remained there. Generations and generations of these rough and independent people remained on the move, exploring the land, sailing the

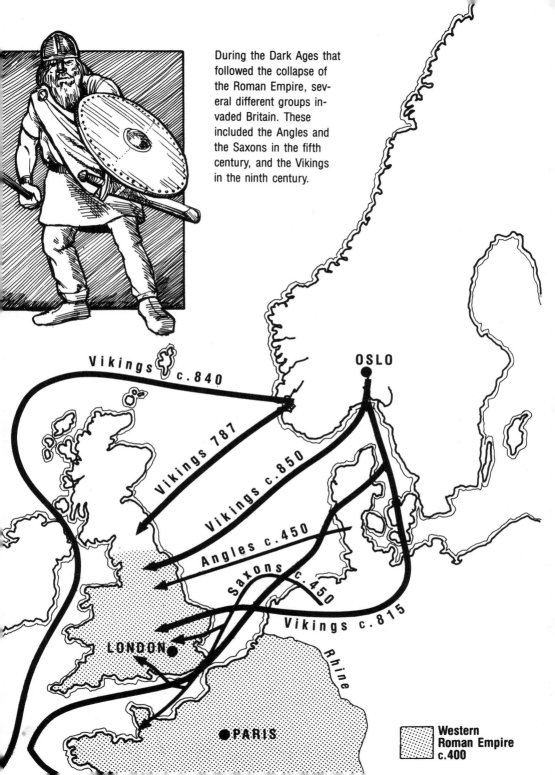

During the Dark Ages that followed the collapse of the Roman Empire, several different groups invaded Britain. These included the Angles and the Saxons in the fifth century, and the Vikings in the ninth century.

OSLO

Vikings c.840

Vikings 787

Vikings c.850

Angles c.450

Saxons c.450

Vikings c.815

Rhine

LONDON

PARIS

Western
Roman Empire
c.400

seas and always, always making war. During the four hundred years Britain was part of the Roman Empire, Rome was getting weaker and weaker, and the Norsemen were getting stronger and stronger. Finally they thundered through the Roman defenses along the northern boundaries of the empire and came howling into Italy and southern Europe.

At the same time the Norsemen were attacking Rome from the north, Mongols, out of Asia, attacked the empire from the east. Rome was really in trouble, for in addition to those attacks they were invaded from the south by the Moslems, who came from North Africa and the Middle East. The Moslems surged across the Mediterranean Sea and occupied southern Italy and Spain. Being attacked on all sides, Rome had to call back her armies from the farthest edges of her empire to protect what was left of the empire at the center, in Italy. By A.D. 409, Rome had lost all control of Britain.

As soon as the Roman armies pulled out of Britain, the Picts and Scots crashed through Hadrian's Wall and began to destroy the Celts. Having spent four hundred years under protection of the Roman army, the Celts were left utterly alone and defenseless. They turned for help to the Angles and Saxons across the sea in Sweden and Denmark. The Celts and the Angles and Saxons already had some knowledge of each other, you remember, because they had been trading. The Angles and Saxons were quick to respond, because they loved war. They did save the Celts from the Picts and Scots; then they turned on the Celts and destroyed practically all the culture which had been brought by the Romans: literature, sculpture, schools and roads. Some traces of Latin words remained in the Celtic speech, but Latin would not return to Britain as an important influence until four hundred years later, during the ninth century, only to be overwhelmed once more by the languages of more Germanic invaders, as we will see in the next chapter.

Once they had destroyed everything in sight, some of the Angles and Saxons returned to their homeland. Others preferred the green fields and milder climate of England to the icy shores of the land of their birth, and they stayed. Eventually, they settled down and became peaceful farmers. Celts, Picts and Scots who had survived the war moved away from these foreign settlers and made their homes in what is now known as Wales, Ireland and Scotland. The Celtic and Scottish languages developed into Welsh, Irish and Scottish Gaelic. Still spoken by a few people in Britain today, these languages are fast disappearing and have no relationship to modern English. The Germanic languages of the Angles and Saxons combined to become Anglo-Saxon. Since the Angles and Saxons had become the power in England, the Anglo-Saxon language became the very early beginning of English.

5

OLD ENGLISH

While the Anglo-Saxons were establishing their power in England and making their language the main language of that country, over on the continent of Europe the Roman Empire was sinking deeper and deeper into trouble. Rome continued to be attacked from all sides—by the Germanic peoples of the north, the Mongols from the east and the Moslems from the south—for the next five hundred years. The invasions came so fast and from so many directions that by A.D. 476 the western empire, the part that was in southern and central Europe and had its headquarters in Rome, had ceased to exist. And since the Germanic peoples, who had conquered Rome from the north, had no interest in preserving Roman culture, it just died.

This is the period of European history known as the Dark Ages. Roman roads wore away. Buildings crumbled. The art works and books which had not already been slashed and burned by the Northmen dwindled to dust. Land which had been unified under the law and government of one gigantic empire split apart into separate armed camps, called feudal estates, each with a law and government of its own. Since the Roman roads were worn away, the cities died, and all trade ceased. Each feudal estate had to grow and manufacture every-thing it needed for itself. Since there was much unclaimed land between the estates, and no centralized law or government to control it, the estates were at constant war with each other over territory. Each estate walled itself off from its enemies. Anyone venturing outside these walls was at the mercy of roving bands of outlaws who made their living by robbery and murder. In general, life in those days was short and harsh and nasty.

Walled off from each other as they were, the people of Europe lost contact with each other. Their languages began to change from Latin, the language of the Roman Empire, into what is now known as Italian, Spanish, Portuguese, French and German. Italian, Spanish and Portuguese are the closest to Latin. French is a combination of Germanic languages and Latin, and German is closest to the language of the Norsemen.

At this time, about the only thing the European people had in common was Christianity. What little was left of Roman culture and the Latin language was saved by the Church. What little law and order was left among the separate feudal estates was provided by the Church. The Church was all that was left of Roman civilization, and even there, the greatness of Rome was only a memory. But Latin survived as the language of church-men and the wealthy, educated classes, and was to have a pro-found effect on the development of the languages of southern Europe and England.

Gradually, between the sixth and eleventh centuries, the feudal estates grew into powerful kingdoms. Of these, the French kingdom of Normandy became very important to the development of English.

The various peoples in England were coming together as a nation also, under the rule of more powerful kings such as Alfred the Great, who ruled between 871 and 899. Alfred was not only an efficient ruler and a great defender of his people, he was also an eager scholar. He was able to preserve some of the learning which had been left behind when the Romans left

England. During his rule, Christian missionaries from the Church in Europe visited England, bringing with them Latin and more Roman culture. Alfred learned Latin so that he could translate ancient writings into Anglo-Saxon. In Anglo-Saxon he began a detailed diary of events in his own time known as *The Anglo-Saxon Chronicle*. Although Alfred encouraged reading and writing in Anglo-Saxon as well as in Latin, most works continued to be written in Latin.

Alfred's efforts to unify England and establish a national language apart from Latin were interrupted by an invasion of yet another group of Norsemen, the Vikings. A wild, adventurous, seagoing people, the Vikings are believed to have explored as far as the shores of North America long before Columbus. They came from the shores of what is now Denmark and Holland, and they invaded England and France over a thousand years ago. The Vikings who invaded England were called Danes, and those who invaded France were known as the Normans.

In England, Alfred was able to defend the western part of the land against the Danes, but they took full control of the east. Writings in Anglo-Saxon continued to show Latin influence clear into the tenth century. A tenth-century Anglo-Saxon king, Eadred, described himself in this way: *Angul-Seaxna cyning and Casere toitus Brittaniae*. The first half of that phrase is Anglo-Saxon and the second is Latin. It means: "King of the Anglo-Saxons and Caesar of all Britain." *Cyning* is the Anglo-Saxon ancestor of the Modern English king.

Gradually, as all invaders do eventually, the Danes settled down. Their descendants became peaceful farmers. Their language mixed with Anglo-Saxon and became what we know as Old English. At that time, Latin influence on the language all but disappeared.

Here are some English words written with modern spelling which come directly from the language of the Vikings: both, though, until, sky, fellow, skin, scrap, steak. The very important

English word "law" comes directly from the Danish Vikings. In their language it was *log*, which meant "that which is laid down" (we lay down the law). In Old English the word became *lagu*, and from that came the Modern English law.

A great deal more was to happen to English words before they took on the form and spelling they have today. But you can see the early influence of the Danes when you look at the first line of an old rhyme from Friesland. (Friesland is a part of Holland, which was one of the homes of the Vikings. In present day Holland the language is Dutch.) The line is: *Brod, butter en grene chiese*. This is hardly different at all from modern Dutch or Modern English: "Bread, butter and green cheese." Today, the English and Dutch languages are considered very close cousins, although their pronunciations are very different from each other.

Anglo-Saxon, the other strong influence on English, was probably quite a different sounding language from either Dutch or modern English. But even so, once it is translated, you can see where many of today's words come from. Here are a few lines from the Lord's Prayer in Anglo-Saxon. It was written in the ninth century. See if you can guess which lines they are.

> Fæder ūre, þū ðe eartpōn heofunum
> si in nama gahalgod
> ......
> And forgyf ūs ūre gyltas
> swā swā wē forgyfaþ ūrum gyltendum.

If you were to translate these lines into a modern English which is closest to the Anglo-Saxon, it might look something like this:

> Father our, thou that art on heavens
> Be thy name godly
> ......
> And forgive us our guilts
> So so we forgive our guiltings

And finally, when you translate it into the English of today, you find that the lines are:

Our Father, who art in heaven,
Hallowed be thy name
......
Forgive us our trespasses
As we forgive those who trespass against us.

Old English was established as the language of the land by the tenth century. For the next hundred years or so after the Danish invasions, the English people lived in peace. If they had continued that way our language today might be quite different from what it is; it would be something similar to Dutch, Danish and German. But about nine hundred years ago, England was invaded again, and another, very different language was brought to the country. When this language arrived, English moved away from Danish and Anglo-Saxon and passed from Old English into Middle English.

6

MIDDLE ENGLISH

The new foreign language which was to have such an important influence on the development of Middle English was French. While generations of Danes were living in England, and the Anglo-Saxon language was mixing with theirs and becoming Old English, generations of Normans, also descendants of Vikings, were living in France. The Frankish-Latin language of the French was slowly becoming Norman French, which is known as Old French. Old French and Old English were as foreign to each other as modern forms of those languages are today. In 1066, the Norman French people invaded England. The invasion is known as the Norman Conquest, and it is very important for two reasons. First, it was the last time England was ever to be invaded. Second, Old French became as important an influence as Danish and Anglo-Saxon to the development of English as it is today.

The Normans brought their law, customs and literature to England. Since there was still so much Latin in their own language, Latin again began to have an influence on English. But this time, the English people did not allow their language to be swallowed up by a foreign language in the way their Celtic and early Anglo-Saxon ancestors had. Although the invading Norman French became the rulers of the land, and French became the language of government and law in England, the English people stubbornly refused to give up their own language. English remained the spoken language of the people. And when they did accept French words, they mispronounced them so badly that no one could recognize them as French.

Here is a sample of writing from 1340, well into the Middle English period. It is remarkable, because it contains no French words. It is much closer to the Anglo-Saxon of the ninth century. How|much|can|you |understand? |Hints: |The symbol þ stood for the *th* sound. *Y-wyte* was an early word meaning "know." The *ou* here is pronounced like the *ou* in *about*. The modern English word meaning relatives or family is *kin*. Kent is an area of England. The letter *v* is pronounced like *f*. Now read:

> Nou ich wille þet ye y-wyte houhit is y-went
> þet þis boc is y-write mid engliss of Kent
> ......
> vor fader, and vor moder and vor oþer ken.

You could translate it something like this:

> Now I will that you know how it is gone
> That this book is written with English of Kent
> ......
> For father, and for mother and for other kin.

In the English of today, it can be translated like this:

> Now I want you to know how it goes:
> That this book is written in the English of Kent
> ......
> For father, and for mother and for other relatives.

So, for a time, England was a land where there were two languages—the French of the ruling class, and the Anglo-Saxon, or Old English, of the servant class, the English people. Smart people of both classes learned both languages, and eventually the two languages came together to form what we know today as Middle English. Middle English was neither French nor Anglo-Saxon; it was a completely different language combined of both. The change from Old English to Middle English took place gradually over a period of about three hundred years.

By looking at some everyday modern English words we can see which were originally the French ruling class words and which were the English peasant or working class words. Because after the Norman Conquest the kings, lords, and high church officials were all French, modern English words in government, law, religion, the military, art and learning come mainly from French rather than Anglo-Saxon. The following words all come from French:

Government Words		*Law Words*	*Religious Words*
crown	tax	crime	sermon
state	office	proof	pray
reign	major	bail	lesson
royal	prince	fine	pastor
court		prison	saint
parliament		arrest	faith
assembly		arson	mercy
		fraud	preach

Military Words	*Fashion Words*	*Art and Learning Words*
army	fashion	sculpture
navy	gown	beauty
peace	fur	color
battle	jewel	poetry

(continued on p. 30)

Military Words	Fashion Words	Art and Learning Words
siege	robe	study
soldier	coat	grammar
spy	collar	medicine
conquer		paper
		pen
		copy

Since the peasants, servants and hunters were English, modern English words of farms, housework and the outdoors come from Anglo-Saxon rather than French. Here are some examples: flesh, meat, corn, fish, milk, cow, pig, deer, sheep, spider, wasp, beetle.

The French ruling class lived in grand homes, often castles, and the English peasants and other workers lived in poor huts of wood and straw. So modern English words for the simple, basic things in a household come from Anglo-Saxon, and the finer, more luxurious things come from the French.

Old English	Old French
home	curtain
house	screen
room	parlor
window	chamber
door	pantry
hearth	chimney
floor	porch

The English people gradually accepted more and more French words. Sometimes they chose to use the French word for something and forgot all about the Anglo-Saxon word. Often they used words from both languages for the same thing, as in the case of room, which is Anglo-Saxon, and chamber, which is French. But just as often, they held fast to their old Anglo-Saxon forms, refusing to accept the French at all. So, today, some of our simplest, most important words are traced back not to the French ruling class, but to the Anglo-Saxon working class. Most of our "grammar" words, that is, those words that connect all other words in a sentence, are Anglo-Saxon. Here are some examples:

Verbs	Prepositions	Conjunctions	Adverbs
live	of	and	here
die	to	but	there
come	by	if	where
go	for		when
make	from		how
give	in		
take	at		
eat	on		
dunk	under		
work			
play			

Without using grammar words like these, it is impossible to form a complete sentence or express a complete idea. Let's take a few words from the lists of words from the French and try to make a sentence with them: royal prince battle pray faith mercy. No matter in what order you arrange these words, you cannot get a sensible sentence; there is no idea expressed at all by these words alone. You need some grammar words to connect the other words in a sensible way. Let's add the Anglo-Saxon: when the goes to he for and. Now let's arrange these words in a pattern with the French words: When the royal prince goes to battle he prays for faith and mercy. Since most of our grammar words are of Anglo-Saxon origin, linguists say that English has a vocabulary which is mainly French, and a grammar which is almost entirely Anglo-Saxon.

Generations of Normans intermarried with the Anglo-

Saxon people. The Anglo-Saxons rose to high positions in government, and England became a powerful nation, independent of France and of all other influence. People of French ancestry no longer considered themselves French. There had been so much intermarriage that there was no longer a strong distinction between French and Anglo-Saxon. There was still a wealthy ruling class and a poor working class, but the ruling class was not all French, and the working class not all Anglo-Saxon. The two peoples had mixed, and all classes were English.

Geoffrey Chaucer was the greatest writer of Middle English. His famous work, *Canterbury Tales,* was written around 1387, three hundred years after the Norman Conquest and some six hundred years before our own time, but it is still read today. It is the story of a group of travelers, or pilgrims, who made a journey to the city of Canterbury to visit the cathedral where an archbishop had been murdered by knights who served King Henry II of England. On the way, each pilgrim tells a story to pass the time. In the first few lines, which are quoted below, Chaucer introduces the stories by saying that when April comes, with its showers and mild weather, people feel like traveling. You can see both the French and the Anglo-Saxon influences in the writing. Some of the words, like *Aprille, veyne, licour, vertu, engendered* and *pilgrimages,* are from French. *Veyne* is the vein of a leaf; *vertu* is virtue; *licour* can mean liquor or liquid, but Chaucer uses it to mean moisture; and *engendered* means born. Anglo-Saxon words are: *whan, thanne, that, droghte, and, folk, to, on.* Many of the words are the same as they are today. See how much of this you can understand:

> Whan that Aprille with his shoures soote
> The droghte of March hath perced to the roote,
> And bathed every veyne in swich licour
> Of which vertu engendered is the flour;
> ......
> thanne longen folk to goon on pilgrimages

Chaucer wrote the whole work in the form of a poem. If we are to get the meaning of all his words, we have to translate the verses into sentences, because once we change the spelling into the modern form, the words no longer rhyme. The result is something not nearly as beautiful as Chaucer's poem, but it helps us to understand what he wrote. A translation could be something like this:

> When that April with his sweet showers has pierced to the root the drought of March, and bathed every vein in such moisture of which virtue the flower is born . . . then folk long to go on pilgrimages.

During the period of time in which Middle English became Modern English, the language continued to change, but the changes were internal; that is, there was no more outside influence on the language brought by foreign invaders. After 1066, England was never invaded again.

7

MODERN ENGLISH

There was fairly little written literature during the Middle English period. Except for the works of Chaucer, which were in a language closer to that of the people, most literature was in Latin or French. Most people couldn't read anyway, and even for those who could read and write, there were no spellers, dictionaries or grammar books with rules to keep the language in order. In the absence of rule books, which few could have read in any case, people tended to pronounce words any old way, the easiest way, and they made up new words as it suited them. Also, the accents of the people in northern, southern and central England varied widely. Words could be spelled the way they sounded, but they sounded so different to so many different writers, that spelling was just about what anyone wanted it to be. Even today, English spelling does not always make too much sense.

To make matters worse, during the Middle English period, some scholars wanted to give English Latin grammar or French spelling, in spite of the fact that these were very different from English speech. When we speak of the grammar of a language we mean, among other things, the order in which words are arranged in a sentence. In Latin, words are often arranged in a pattern which is very different from English patterns. As an example let's look at the words of an ancient Roman humorist. He described man as no more than a "two-legged animal without feathers." In Latin that phrase is *animal bipes implume.* If we substitute English words but keep the Latin grammar we get: "animal two-legged unfeathered." With Latin words the pattern is smooth and sensible, but in English it seems awkward and silly.

As for French spelling, we still use it for many English words today, such as bureau, guy, maneuver, rendezvous and restaurant, but we pronounce the words differently from the French. In Chaucer's time there were even more French spellings. Look back at the lines *Aprille, shoures, vertu* and *flour* from *Canterbury Tales.* As you know, these have changed to April, showers, virtue and flower, bringing them closer to the sounds of the English tongue.

So you can see that Middle English was a very disorganized language. But in Europe and in the Middle East, many changes were taking place which would have an important effect on the future of the English language. Let's look back for a moment to see what these changes were.

In the fifth century A.D. the Roman Empire had split into the western and eastern empires. The western empire, with its capital in Rome, fell when the Germanic peoples invaded from the north and the Moslems from across the Mediterranean Sea in the south. The eastern empire, based in Constantinople, continued to enjoy the superior culture and learning of Greece and Rome and the Moslem Arabs for another thousand years after western Rome was defeated and Europe fell into the Dark Ages. As western Europe split into feudal estates the Moslems of the Middle East were pushing farther west and threatening the Christian rulers of the eastern empire.

The Moslems had captured Jerusalem, in the Holy Land in 638. European kings wanted it back, because they felt it belonged to Christians. They broke through the Moslem defenses along the Mediterranean Sea and sailed east to begin a long series of wars called the Crusades. For two hundred years, from 1095 to 1291, European Christians joined forces with Middle Eastern Christians against the Moslems and fought battles along the coast of North Africa and in the areas which are known today as Turkey, Iran, Iraq, Lebanon, Syria, Israel, Saudi Arabia and other Middle Eastern nations. At the end of that time, Europe was able to occupy some parts of North Africa, Greece and Turkey, but the rest of the Middle East remained in the hands of the Moslems. Religion and culture remained Moslem, and the languages spoken in those areas were Iranian and Arabic.

In terms of capturing territory or spreading the Christian religion in the Middle East, Europe lost the wars of the Crusades. But the Crusades had brought the Europeans back into contact with the superior ancient Greek and Roman cultures, and those cultures had been enriched by the Moslem's advanced knowledge of mathematics, astronomy, geography and medicine.

This renewed contact with all the knowledge which had been lost during the Dark Ages marks the beginning of a period in Europe known as the Renaissance, which means "re-birth of learning." The lost works of ancient Greek and Roman writers were rediscovered in Europe, inspiring countless new works of literature, art and science. The Renaissance began in Italy, but eventually the new learning spread north, to France, Germany and England.

Geoffrey Chaucer was born some hundred years after the last war of the Crusades, in the early part of the Renaissance. About one hundred fifty years after Chaucer's death William Shakespeare was born, in the last part of the Renaissance. During the lifetimes of these two great writers and over all the years between, the English language was sorting itself out from the chaos of Middle English. By the time of Shakespeare's death in 1616, our history and our language had entered the modern period.

During the Renaissance there was so much excitement over the new ideas, discoveries and inventions that more and more people were learning to read and write in order to learn more. The printing press was invented in Germany and brought to England. A man named William Caxton was the first English printer, and because of his machine, books in England became cheaper and more plentiful. Some thoughtful writers began to put together dictionaries and grammar books, and these books began to establish certain standards for how words should be spelled, pronounced and put together in a sentence.

William Shakespeare wrote thirty-eight plays and well over one hundred fifty poems. He wrote about ancient Romans and Greeks, about kings and queens of England who lived hundreds of years before his own lifetime, and about people and places far, far from England. He was able to do so because of the rediscoveries of old writings which were coming into England throughout the Renaissance. For the play *Julius Caesar,* which is quoted below, Shakespeare got his information from the works of an ancient Roman called Plutarch, who lived fourteen hundred years before Shakespeare was born! Now, Shakespeare was an educated man, and could read and translate Plutarch's Latin into English. During his time there were many more people who could read and write than ever before, but we must remember that most people still could not. It would be three or four hundred years before education was available to everyone. So, Shakespeare did not write his plays for people to read, he wrote them for people to watch, and his characters, whether they were ancient Roman emperors, Egyptian queens, or a prince of Denmark, spoke in the language of the English people. The English of Shakespeare's time is considered modern English because, except for some different spellings and a few words we no longer use, the language is quite similar to the English we speak today. Many of the old sayings we use every day come right out of Shakespeare's writings. When we think something is unimportant we "laugh it off." Describing something which is strong and in good condition, we say it is "sound as a bell." When we are disgusted with something, we say it is "lousy." If you know or use these expressions you are quoting Shakespeare.

Here is an extract from Shakespeare's *Julius Caesar*. Julius Caesar was a great emperor of Rome, and the Roman people loved him. However, there were other powerful men of the empire who felt that he was not the best man for the job of emperor. Besides, they were jealous of him and wanted more power for themselves. So they plotted to kill him. Their plot succeeded, and on the day of March fifteenth, he was stabbed to death in a public square.

In the scene below, Caesar is walking among cheering crowds with the men who eventually kill him. He thinks they are his friends. Their names are Casca, Cassius and Brutus. A soothsayer, a man who can tell the future, bursts out of the crowd and tries to warn Caesar of what will happen on March fifteenth. In ancient Rome that time of that month was called the Ides of March. Caesar listens to the soothsayer but does not believe what he says. Here is how Shakespeare tells us it all happened.

SOOTHSAYER: Caesar!

CAESAR: Ha! Who calls?

CASCA: Bid every noise be still: peace yet again!

CAESAR: Who is it in the press that calls on me? I hear a tongue, shriller than all the music, Cry 'Caesar.' Speak; Caesar is turn'd to hear.

SOOTHSAYER: Beware the Ides of March.

CAESAR: What man is that?

BRUTUS:	A soothsayer bids you beware the Ides of March.
CAESAR:	Set him before me; let me see his face.
CASSIUS:	Fellow, come from the throng; look upon Caesar.
CAESAR:	What say'st thou to me now? Speak once again.
SOOTHSAYER:	Beware the Ides of March.
CAESAR:	He is a dreamer; let us leave him. Pass.

Although the language of Shakespeare is considered modern English, it is still quite different from twentieth-century American English, and when we read his works, we need instruction and explanation. But you can see in the passage above that most of the words are very easy for us to understand. It is easy to see how much the English of Shakespeare's time had changed from Chaucer's English. Compare this passage with the one from Chaucer's *Canterbury Tales* on page 32. After Shakespeare's time English was to change a great deal more, but the changes were gradual. The changes came as a result of the growth of the English Empire, advancements in transportation and communication and a continuing contact between English-speaking peoples and peoples from all parts of the world.

Between the sixteenth and nineteenth centuries England built an empire which included North America, some Caribbean islands, Australia, New Zealand, parts of Asia and parts of Africa. About nine or ten years before Shakespeare's death, England had established her first American colony, Virginia. Three hundred years later, England no longer had an empire, but the lands which she had conquered still spoke the English language. Today, English is the native or official language of not only the United States but Canada, Australia, New Zealand, India, Hong Kong, Kenya, South Africa, Trinidad, Jamaica, and more—lands on every continent of this planet.

It has been said that English is four-fifths a combination of Anglo-Saxon, Germanic and French, and one-fifth everything else. In the next chapters we will explore that "everything else." We have seen that English has gone through such a long and complicated series of changes that what we speak today is a language entirely different from its ancestors. Then, when English spread over the world it grew and was enriched by words borrowed from many other languages. Borrowed words are a very large part of that "one-fifth everything else."

8

BORROWED WORDS
· · ·

There are 2,796 languages spoken in the world today, and English has borrowed words from a great many of them. The Chinese language is spoken by more people than any other. This is because there are a lot of Chinese. The second most spoken language is English. This is *not* because there are a lot of English people; as a matter of fact, the population of England is rather small. China has the largest population of the whole world, but the Chinese language has stayed mostly in China, and few non-Chinese ever learn to speak it. English, on the other hand, has spread over the whole world and is spoken by non-English people almost everywhere. Wherever English went it borrowed words from other languages. When foreign languages came to English-speaking countries, English borrowed again. The borrowing began hundreds of years ago and continues to this day.

During the wars of the Crusades, Europeans came into contact with a superior culture which included many advanced ideas in science and mathematics, as well as fascinating customs, delicious food, rich furnishings, weird animals and strange lands. Soldiers returning from the Crusades had many wonders

Although Chinese has the most speakers of all the world's languages, it is confined to China. English is the most widely spread language, with speakers on every continent. Spanish, which is spoken in many South American countries, is also widely spread.

42

English as a first language: *350 million people*

English as a second language: *400 million people*

Spanish: *300 million people*

Chinese: *one billion people*

Russian: *285 million people*

to show and many exciting stories to tell. With all this new knowledge came many Arabic and Persian words, such as algebra, bazaar, candy, caravan, jackal, jungle, khaki, magazine, sofa and sugar.

Here is a list of historical events and periods of migration after the Crusades, during which hundreds of words were borrowed by English-speaking people. Beside each event is a list of languages that contributed new words to English.

Period	Event	Languages
14th to 17th centuries	Renaissance, "rebirth" of learning	Latin, Greek, Romance languages*, German
15th to 16th centuries	European colonization of the Americas	North American Indian, South American Indian, West Indian, Spanish, Dutch, Portuguese, French
17th to 19th centuries	British conquest of parts of Asia and East India	East Indian, Chinese, Japanese
19th century	Slavery in America and West Indies	African languages
19th century	U.S. war with Mexico	Spanish, Mexican, Mexican Indian
19th century	U.S. westward movement	North American Indian, Chinese
17th to 19th centuries	Immigration of Europeans and Chinese to U.S.	All European languages, Chinese
20th century	World Wars I and II	Languages of the whole planet

*The Romance languages are Italian, French, Spanish and Portugese. See page 11.

44

There are three types of language from which English borrows words: languages which have no writing, such as the North American Indian; languages whose alphabets are different from ours, such as Chinese or Arabic; and languages whose alphabet, the Roman alphabet, is like ours, but which are difficult for us to pronounce, such as French or Italian. In the case of the first two types of language we have to put what we think is the sound of the word into the Roman alphabet.

In the case of the third type, we do one of two things. We might keep the foreign spelling, but give it English pronunciation, as in the case of chocolate. Chocolate is a Mexican Indian word which comes to us by way of Spanish. In Spanish it is pronounced cho-ko-LA-tay. In English we say something like CHAW-klut. The other thing we do with foreign words is change the spelling so that it fits English pronunciation. Such is the case with radish, which comes from Italian. In Italian radish is spelled *radice* and pronounced RAH-dee-chee. The first English-speaking person who ever heard that word probably gave the *ice* at the end an *ish* sound, and so the English spelling of the word was changed to *radish.*

All of this borrowing and changes in spelling and pronunciation help to explain why English words are seldom spelled the way they sound. Actually among the world's written languages, English has the most mixed up spelling of all.

Below is a small sample of English words we have borrowed from other languages. They have come into English at different times throughout its history. Some words are still spelled exactly as they are in their original language. These are shown in **bold** type. You can see that English has borrowed from languages of countries on every continent on earth.

Latin and Greek

alibi	**exit**	propaganda	**bonus**
extra	**veto**	cosmos	psychology

45

French

gourmet	beef	biscuit	grape
saucer	dinner	veal	cream
cherry	plate	supper	pork
salad	stew	**rendezvous**	gravy
fruit	fry	**restaurant**	**garage**
bureau			

Italian

piano	**ghetto**	**studio**	radish
cartoon	**spaghetti**	**stanza**	**opera**
chicory	carnival	**malaria**	**broccoli**
cash	medal	**influenza**	**marina**
sentinel	gallop		

German

swindler	halt	**kindergarten**	yodel
blitz	**sauerkraut**	plunder	poodle
poker	**dirndl**		

Dutch/Flemish/Friesian/South African

schooner	sleigh	waffle	**kraal**
Santa Claus	furlough	toy	**dollar**

Spanish/Portuguese

rodeo	sherry	stampede	**tornado**
commando	cockroach	**cargo**	

Spanish (by way of Mexico)

mesa	**adobe**	**patio**	**plaza**

Irish/Scottish/Welch

colleen	plaid	flannel

Slavic (Russian, Polish, Yugoslavian, Czechoslovakian, etc.)

czar (tsar)	vodka	steppe	pogrom

Arabic/Persian

algebra	assassin	syrup	sofa
magazine	safari	bazaar	caravan
jackal	jungle	khaki	candy
lemon	spinach	sugar	

Hebrew

camel	ebony	rabbi	kibbutz
sabra			

Indian (Hindi, Urdu, etc.)

punch	coolie	bandanna	bungalow
calico	polo	dungaree	

Chinese

tea	tycoon	yen

African languages

gorilla	voodoo	zebra	jazz

Mexican Indian languages (by way of Spanish and Portuguese)

chocolate	tomato	coyote

West Indian languages (by way of Spanish, Portuguese, French)

mahogany	cannibal	barbecue	hurricane
potato	tobacco		

South American Indian languages (by way of Spanish)

llama	pampa	jaguar	tapioca

Australian and South Pacific languages

kangaroo	boomerang	atoll	boondock
taboo			

North American Indian languages

There are many North American words in English, but not as many as one might think, and what words there are come to us in a form far different from the original language. There are several reasons why this is true. So North American words deserve a separate chapter of their own.

9

NORTH AMERICAN INDIAN WORDS
• • •

Most white settlers had little interest in the language and culture of the native Americans. Europeans coming to colonize the land in America generally considered Indian ways savage and frightening; they were suspicious of anything "un-Christian." As a result, they not only ignored Indian culture, they set out to destroy it, just as completely as the Germanic invaders had destroyed the culture of the Roman Empire during the Dark Ages in Europe.

But ignorance, fear and hatred of Indian ways are not the only reasons there are not more North American Indian words in American English. Not all Europeans were uninterested in Indian ways. The early settlers in Massachusetts and Virginia lived in peace with the Indians, shared the land, and learned much from them about how to survive in that wild countryside. Some settlers tried to translate Indian languages into English, but they had little success.

For one thing, Indian languages had no written form. Translators had to rely on what they thought were sounds of Indian words and try to put those sounds into the Roman alphabet. This proved to be a nearly impossible task. Indian words were extremely difficult for Europeans to pronounce. Also, Indian languages varied widely from tribe to tribe. Different tribes used sign language to communicate with one another, as well as with white settlers.

Pronunciation was not the only problem. The other problem was the *way* Indians name things. They do not give a single word to a thing or an idea as Europeans do. In English, for example, love is love, thought is thought, water is water, tree is tree, cat is cat, and so on. But in Indian languages, at least according to the European's understanding, things are named for a whole series of ideas connected with them. Indians will use several words instead of only one to describe what the thing does, where it has been, or what it used to be. If this sounds confusing, that's because it is confusing. As it turned out for these early European translators, there were no words in English to translate the exact meanings Indians gave to their words, and no letters to show the exact pronunciation.

Here is an example of the problems involved in translating Indian languages into English or English into Indian languages. One man who tried to put the Bible into an Indian language came up with a word like this: *nummatchekodtantamoonganunnonoas,* which he said meant "our loves." Here is another: *kodonattotummooetiteaonganunnash.* This word, we are to understand, means "our questions."

Not all words, of course, were quite that long, but even translations of shorter ones show white people's problem pronouncing Indian sounds and understanding Indian meanings. Here are two different Indian words for raccoon. In one language it seemed to be *raugraoughcun,* which became *rarowcun,* and finally raccoon. The word was translated as "scratcher." Anyone who has seen a raccoon at work can see the logic in that; the animal was named for what it does. So in this case the meaning of the word is no mystery to a speaker of English. However, in another Indian language the word for raccoon was translated as "a shell it was." This presents quite a mystery until we learn that in this case the animal was not named for what it did, but for what it had been. The rings on the tail of a raccoon, and the black "mask" around its eyes looked to the Indians like the marks on a seashell, and they believed the raccoon had been a shell in a previous existence.

Tomahawk comes from *taccahacan* or *tamahaas,* or *tahmahgan,* and was named for what it does: "a beating thing." Squash, skunk, tuxedo, moccasin, hominy and mackinaw are some other words borrowed from Indian languages, but most of the Indian words which have remained in English are names of places. Many of the names of our states, cities, towns, roads, mountain ranges, rivers and forests have English versions of the old Indian names. Most of these names are beautiful in both sound and meaning. Read these aloud and hear the rhythm: Susquehanna, Rappahannock, Massachusetts, Ohio. The sounds and meanings of Indian place names show us the Indians' lasting love and deep respect for their land. Massachusetts means "place of the great hills." Ohio means "beautiful water." One of the loveliest of all is the name of the river, Shenandoah, which means "daughter of the skies."

10

INVENTED AND OTHER WORDS
• • •

Scholars guess that English has about 600,000 words, but there are probably more. New words continue to come into our language at such a rate that no dictionary could possibly keep up with them. The old words which were born centuries ago in the Anglo-Saxon, Germanic and French languages make up four fifths of the English language. The other one fifth is made up partly of borrowed words and partly of three other kinds of words: words from the names of peoples and places; imitative words; and invented words.

Ampere, volt and watt are all units of electricity, and they are named for the men who discovered them: André M. Ampere, a French physicist; Alessandro Volta, an Italian physicist; and James Watt, a Scottish engineer and inventor. A chesterfield can be either an overcoat or a special kind of couch. Both of these things are named for Lord Chesterfield, who lived in England during the nineteenth century. Nowadays we all drink pasteurized milk, that is, milk which is clean and purified. Pasteurized gets its name from Louis Pasteur, a French doctor who invented the process for purifying milk. There are many words like this in our language and you can read about more of them in Part Two of this book.

Imitative words are words that sound like the thing or action they stand for. Here are some examples:

buzz	click	titter	gargle	bang	growl	mumble
clatter	giggle	boom	chirp	gulp	snarl	bawl
crash	hum	sputter	clap	whine	mutter	

There is no need to say anything else about these words, for they speak for themselves. You can probably think of many more.

Then there are the invented words. English-speaking people have always made up words as it suited them, and they continue to do so every day. One kind of invented word is one which is made up of two other words. Dictionaries call this kind of word a compound. If you put "play" and "thing" together you get the compound, "plaything." How many can you add to this list?

raincoat	milkshake	upstairs	standstill	headlight
shutout	gocart	sailboat	downstairs	income
override	headline			

As well as putting two whole words together, we also add parts of words called prefixes and suffixes to whole words. Most prefixes and suffixes come from Latin or Greek, and each has a special meaning of its own. When we add a prefix before a word or a suffix at the end of it, we change its meaning. For example, the prefix re- means "again." If we add re- to do or paint, we get two new words meaning "do again" and "paint again." Un- means "the opposite of" or "not." By adding un to happy or kind we get unhappy or unkind, meaning "not happy" and "not kind." The suffix -ness means "the condition of." Happiness and kindness are the conditions of being happy and kind. It is easy

53

to see the meanings of unhappiness and unkindness. The word to which we attach the prefixes and suffixes is called the root word. In a word like unkindness the root word is kind.

Some words, like astronaut, are made up entirely of Greek or Latin prefixes and suffixes. *Astro-* is a Greek prefix meaning having to do with the stars; *naut-* means having to do with sailing. So, an *astronaut* is a "star-sailor." Other words can be root words, prefixes or suffixes, depending on where they come in the word. Remember, the prefix comes first, the root word second, and the suffix last. As an example, let's take the word "graph" and build several different invented words with it by adding prefixes and suffixes to it or using it as a prefix or suffix. Graph by itself means anything which is shown to us in pictures or writing. For instance, your teacher might want to keep track of your reading progress by drawing a graph of your reading test scores, or a businessman might draw graphs which show the ups and downs of his company's sales records.

Now, by adding the prefixes and suffixes listed below to graph we can make several new words. Notice that graph is part of a longer suffix as well as a suffix by itself.

Prefixes		*Suffixes*	
auto-	self	-graphy	study of; art of
bio-	life	-graph	something written
phono-	sound	-ic	similar to; like
photo-	light	-ology	study of
tele-	distant	-phone	sound

Here are some words made with graph.
  autograph—signature; a person's name written in his or
    her handwriting
  biography—story of a person's life
  autobiography—study of a person's life written by
    himself or herself
  graphology—study of handwriting

54

telegraph—distant writing
telegraphy—art of using the telegraph machine
phonograph—writing or a picture in sound
photograph—writing or a picture in light
photography—art of taking pictures
graphic—clearly written or drawn

You may have noticed that you can make even other words using some of these prefixes and suffixes without graph. "Biology" is the study of life. What do you think is the meaning of biologic? If the prefix *anti-* means "against," what does antibiotic really mean? There are hundreds of Latin and Greek prefixes in our language, and the possibilities for inventing new words are endless. Every day, as we make new discoveries in science and technology, we invent new words to describe them. Many of these new words are combinations of root words and prefixes and suffixes which have already existed in our language for centuries.

Another kind of invented word is the nonsense word. Some nonsense words are used for a while by only a few people and then disappear completely from the language, never to be used again. Others, when they become popular enough and are used over a period of time, become a permanent part of the language. If enough people decide and agree on the meaning of an invented word, it is here to stay. Some examples of everyday modern words which probably began as nonsense words centuries ago are: bad, big, lad, lass, blob, chat, job and fun. Linguists guess that these are nonsense words because they have not been able to trace them back to any of the ancestor languages. Just who invented them, and when or where remains a puzzle. Puzzle itself is one of these mystery words. No one knows where it came from.

Lewis Carroll, author of *Alice in Wonderland* and *Through the Looking Glass,* was a great inventor of nonsense words. As a matter of fact, he created a whole language of nonsense, called

Jabberwocky after his comical monster, the Jabberwock. Here is part of a poem he wrote about the Jabberwock. The nonsense words in it are in bold type.

> Beware the **Jabberwock**, my son!
>   The jaws that bite, the claws that catch
> Beware the **Jubjub** bird, and shun
>   The **frumious Bandersnatch**
>   ......
> And, as in **uffish** though he stood,
>   The **Jabberwock**, with eyes of flame,
> Came **whiffling** through the **tulgey** wood,
>   And burbled as it came!
>   ......
> "And has thou slain the **Jabberwock?**
>   Come to my arms, my **beamish** boy!
> Oh **frabjous** day! **Callooh! Callay!**"
>   He **chortled** in his joy.

Most of Carroll's nonsense words are not used in English, except for "chortle." Chortle, Carroll tells us, is a cross between a chuckle and a snort. He called words like this *portmanteau* words. *Portmanteau* is the French word for "suitcase." Chortle is a portmanteau word, says Carroll, because "there are two different meanings packed together in it."

But Lewis Carroll was not the first to invent portmanteau words, nor will he be the last. The dictionary calls such words blends, and a common old one is squawk, which is a combination of squall ("to bawl") and squeak. A fairly recent blend, which, unfortunately, we hear almost every day, is "smog," a combination of smoke and fog.

People invent nonsense words by combining certain sounds that just seem to fit the things or actions they describe. Often we make up words for anything which is basically rather silly. Spoof was invented by an English comedian some fifty years ago. It means "to poke fun at." Hornswoggle was used a great deal in the United States during the nineteenth century, and it means "to cheat." If a dishonest politician wants to hornswoggle the taxpayers, he invents a "boondoggle," which is a useless, expensive project which does nobody any good. Fairly recently someone invented the word "gobbledygook." When people talk or write using long, fancy words that really mean nothing, we call it gobbledygook. Unfortunately, many people use gobbledygook because they want to seem more important than they are, or because they don't really want people to understand what they mean or what they are doing. So, when the dishonest politician wants to hornswoggle the public with a boondoggle, he usually explains things in gobbledygook.

When Lewis Carroll was writing his books the word gobbledygook had not been invented yet, but Carroll would have known exactly what it meant. Carroll loved to spoof or poke fun at people who used fancy, important-sounding words when simple language would have done better. In one part of *Through the Looking Glass,* Alice has a conversation with Humpty Dumpty in which Humpty Dumpty insists words can mean whatever he wants them to mean. Alice insists that this is impossible. If everyone did that no one would understand anyone else. The conversation goes like this:

> "But 'glory' doesn't mean 'a nice knockdown argument.'" Alice objected.
> "When *I* use a word," Humpty Dumpty said, in rather a scornful tone, "it means just what I choose it to mean—neither more or less."
> "The question is," said Alice, "whether you *can* make words mean so many different things."
> "The question is," said Humpty Dumpty, "which is to be the master—that's all."

The question *is,* just as Humpty Dumpty said, which is to be master. But Humpty Dumpty used words any old way, and that made him a master of gobbledygook, not a master of language. A master of language knows what words really mean, and where they come from; knows when to use big, important ones and when to use the shorter, equally important simple ones. Winston Churchill was a great British prime minister. He was also a great writer, truly a master of language. He said once, "Short words are best, and old words when they are short, are best of all." The stories in the next section are about all kinds of words—old, new, long and short.

PART

TWO.

WORD
STORIES

11

BORROWED WORDS

Assassin/Assassination

Definition: Assassination is a secretly planned murder. Assassins work in groups or alone. Some are hired by others, and some do the job by themselves, for their own reasons. The word is borrowed from Arabic.

Hundreds of years ago, in the south of Persia, there lived a man whose name meant terror and death to all who heard it. He was called Sheik-al-jebal, the Old Man of the Mountain. This sheik, or king, was the absolute ruler of his land. He held his power by making sure all his enemies were dead.

He didn't do all this killing by himself, of course. He kept around him a band of men whose only job was to carry out his secret plots of murder. These men would creep like ghosts into a victim's rooms to drop poison into his food. Or, in a more violent mood, with eyes ablaze, they would crash in upon a victim and hack him to pieces with long, razor sharp, curved swords called scimitars. They were monsters indeed, and were spoken of far and wide throughout the Arab world with terror and disgust.

Now, unless a person is evil through and through or totally insane, killing is not an easy business. It is likely that many of the Old Man's monsters came by murder naturally, but is just as likely that many did not. In any case, they had no choice but to obey the Sheik or be killed themselves. So, in order to get the courage to murder and to dull their senses against the pain and bloodshed they caused, they took a drug called hashish.

Hashish comes from a plant which is used to make hemp, the material of rope. It is the leaves which contain the drug. They can be chewed or dried and smoked like tobacco. An extremely dangerous drug, hashish does peculiar things to the brain. It can dull the senses to the point that a person under its influence will behave like a sleepwalker. A person using the drug regularly over a period of time can go wildly insane and behave like a slobbering, vicious animal. Under the influence of hashish, the Old Man's men were able to murder hundreds of people without feeling much fear or pain for themselves.

Because of their habit of chewing hashish, the Old Man's murderers came to be known as *Hashishin,* the "hashish-eaters." During the Crusades, when Europe was trying to recapture the Holy Land from the Arabs, many Europeans came into contact with the Sheik-al-jebal, and many died horribly at the hands of the Hashishin. The English understood the word as assassin, and that is the word we have used ever since for one who carries out a secretly planned murder.

Barbecue/Buccaneer

Definitions: Barbecue is a method of roasting food over an open fire. A buccaneer is a pirate. Both words began as Caribbean or South American Indian words which were mispronounced in various ways, first by the Spanish and Portuguese, then by the French, and finally by the English. Barbecue is fairly close to the original meaning of the word, but buccaneer came to mean something quite different.

Barbecue

When the European explorers came to the Caribbean is-lands and South America they found lands far different from their own. The climate was unbearably hot and sticky, and food spoiled easily. In many places the land was all thick jungle full of wild animals, poisonous snakes and hundreds of crawling sting-ing insects. The European explorers and settlers learned very quickly that their own methods of staying alive were useless in this kind of country. So they copied Indian ways.

On the island of Hispaniola the Indians lived mostly out-doors, but they would never sleep on the ground. There were too many snakes and insects for that. For sleeping they built little platforms on top of a high frame, somewhat like the bunk bed of today. They built a similar structure for preserving food. They preserved meat and fish by drying or smoking. In order to keep the smoking food out of the reach of prowling wild ani-mals they hung it high on a framework made of tree branches. In order to keep the animals away from the food while it was being cooked, they dug pits into the ground and roasted meat and vegetables on hot coals.

It is not clear what the original Indian word was for these inventions but Spanish and Portuguese visitors understood it to be *barbacoa,* and they soon set about making *barbacoas* of their own. When the English came, they took the Spanish word and turned it into barbecue. Today, barbecue has nothing to do with beds, but, as everyone knows, means charcoal-roasting meat in an open brick oven or inside a barbecue pit.

Buccaneer

On other islands in the Caribbean and in parts of South America, other Indians had similar methods for cooking and preserving food. We don't known exactly what their word was for the meat-smoking frame, but French explorers and settlers understood it to be *boucan*. Like the Spanish and Portuguese, the French found it very practical and easy to build, and soon had many *boucans* of their own. Anyone who built one or used one was known as a *boucanier*.

Now at that time pirates roamed everywhere on the high seas, attacking ships coming back from the New World with their rich cargoes of gold and silver. Eventually the pirates landed on the shores of those places where the gold and silver came from. French pirates, coming into contact with the *boucaniers,* began to call themselves by that name. No one knows why, exactly. Perhaps they liked the sound of the word. English pirates must have liked the word, too, because they also called themselves *boucaniers,* but they pronounced the word *buccaneer.*

Over the next three or four hundred years, the original, peaceful meaning of *boucanier* was completely forgotten as buccaneers from all nations continued to terrorize the high seas.

Coconut

Definition: A coconut is the fruit of a palm tree that grows in Asia, Africa, Latin America and other tropical lands. The word—the first part of it, at least—comes from Portuguese.

The coconut grows to the size and shape of a human head. It has a hard brown shell which is covered with thin fibers that look somewhat like dry human hair. At the base of the nut, where it was connected to the stem, are three dots, which look like two eyes and a mouth.

Portuguese explorers discovered coconuts in the fifteenth century on the islands in the South Pacific and Indian oceans. The Portuguese, just like everyone else at that time, believed in witches, goblins and bogeymen, and scared their children half to death with vivid descriptions of them. No one had ever seen these creatures, but they had all heard enough ghost stories to know they would recognize a goblin if they ever saw one. When they came upon the fruit of the palm tree they knew that here at last was the creature of their nightmares—a goblin, with evil little eyes and a twisted up mouth. So they named it *coco*, which in their language means both "grinning face" and "bogeyman."

Dumbbell

Definition: A dumbbell is a metal bar to which heavy balls have been attached at either end. It is used for weight lifting exercises. The word is a combination of two Old German words. Dumbbell can also mean a stupid person. This word comes from a combination of a German or Dutch word and a French word.

Throughout the ages, ever since their invention, bells have been a very important part of village and town life. Bells were rung to mark the time of day, to announce the curfew, to warn the people of danger, to call them to church and town meetings, to celebrate happy events, or to toll the news of a tragedy.

Gradually the art of bell ringing developed from a simple series of ding-dongs to the playing of hymns, Christmas carols and anthems. Proper bell ringing required special training, and while the bell ringers were learning and practicing, the noise was enough to drive the whole town crazy. Then, one day, some clever person hit upon the idea of constructing a bell mechanism with silent bells. With this device, ringers could practice the motions until they got them exactly right, and if they hit the wrong notes, no one could hear them. The device was called a dumb bell. The original meaning of dumb was "silent" and had nothing to do with stupid.

Because of the constant pulling, swinging and stretching involved in bell ringing, bell ringers were well developed in the chest, shoulders and upper arms. The dumb bell began to be used for the purpose of body building as well as practice for bell ringing. After that, any weight used for exercise came to be known as a dumbbell, even though it looked nothing like a church or clockbell.

The word dumb began to mean "stupid" when English speaking people picked up the word *dumbkopf* from the Germans and Dutch. A *dumbkopf* in those languages is a blockhead, a dummy. In English, the word became dumbbell, but the "bell" came from the French *belle,* meaning pretty girl. It might have been used at first to describe a girl who was nice looking but not too bright. *Belle* changed to bell, and dumbbell came to mean anyone who was slow or dull witted.

Easel

Definition: An easel is a three-legged stand which artists use to set their paintings on as they work on them. The word is borrowed from Dutch.

From ancient times to today, people have named objects after their resemblance to animals or parts of animals. A cat's-eye is a jewel which has the color and shine of the eyes of a cat. When we "dogear" the pages of a book, we turn down the corners so that they look like the ears of a terrier. A gooseneck lamp has a long thin neck which can be twisted this way and that, depending on where you want the light.

It is no surprise then, that somewhere during the Middle

Ages carpenters named the supports for the wood they were cutting horses, or sawhorses, as we call them today. These are sturdy, four-legged structures with a broad back to set a log or plank of wood on. Real horses are sturdy, have four legs and a broad back; the supports do look somewhat like a child's drawing of a horse.

In the seventeenth century in Holland, artists invented a three-legged stand to support the canvas they painted on. This was much smaller than the carpenters' horse, and not so sturdy, but it served a similar purpose. It could not be called a horse, exactly, so it was given the name of the horse's smaller cousin, the donkey. In Dutch, donkey is *ezel*. Now, when English artists began to make use of the Dutch invention, they thought it undignified to call a thing that holds a work of art something so lowly as a donkey. In English it sounds ridiculous to say, "The artist stood at his donkey and painted a picture." On the other hand, the Dutch word *ezel* did not sound so silly in English. So, instead of translating *ezel* to "donkey," the English borrowed the word as it was, and changed the spelling to easel.

Filibuster

Definition: A filibuster is a long speech given in Congress in order to block passage of a bill and prevent it from becoming a law. Originally a Dutch word, it was mispronounced in various ways by the French, the Spanish and the English until it took the form it has today. The modern meaning is quite different from the original.

During the years that European nations were colonizing the New World, buccaneers of all nations roamed the seas attacking and stealing from each others' ships. While most pirates called themselves some form of the English buccaneer, the Dutch pirates called themselves *vrijbuiters,* which, in their language, means "free robbers." To the English the word sounded like "freebooter," with the last part sounding like booty, which means "stolen goods." So, English pirates began to be called freebooters as well as buccaneers, and today the word still means pirate.

The French, on the other hand, changed *vrijbuiter* to *fribustier,* and then *flibustier.* The Spanish, hearing that word, changed it to *filibustero,* and the English altered the Spanish word to filibuster.

All words for pirate—buccaneer, freebooter, and filibuster—remained in English long after the days of piracy had vanished. Filibuster, however, came to mean something quite different. No one knows exactly why, but today it has to do with politics.

In the U.S. Congress, laws do not become laws until they are voted on and the majorities in both the House and Senate have approved them. Senators and representatives make speeches for or against the proposed law, or bill, and when all the speeches have been made, the bill is voted on. But Congress keeps a strict schedule, and if all the speeches have not been made by a certain time, the bill is put away for discussion at a later time. The vote is then delayed.

Now, in order to delay the vote some people will make a long, long speech during which nothing can be done about anything. In Congress, the rule is that anyone speaking "has the floor," and cannot be interrupted unless the speaker gives permission. Giving permission is called "yielding (giving up) the floor." A speaker can delay a vote as long as he or she refuses to yield the floor, and by talking as long as he or she pleases on any subject. In an old film called *Mr. Smith Goes to Washington,* Mr. Smith, a senator, held the floor by reciting the Constitution for three days without a break. Such an impossibly long speech is called a filibuster.

We can only guess at why this word was chosen to mean what it does. Perhaps people on the other side of the argument think a filibuster is a kind of piracy, because it weakens their cause and steals their valuable time. Or, it could be merely because of the sound of the word. Pronounce it. It has a sort of windy, explosive sound, and politicians are sometimes known to be windy and explosive.

Marathon

Definition: The marathon is an event in the Olympic Games, a twenty-six mile footrace. The word comes from Greek.

The Olympic Games began in ancient Greece, but it was not until 1896 that the marathon became one of the events. The long race was named after an ancient battle between Athens and Persia.

In 490 B.C. Persia nearly defeated Athens and would have succeeded except for a man named Pheidippides. Seeing how badly things were going for Athens, Pheidippides knew he must go to another Greek city-state, Sparta, for help. He ran the 150 miles between Athens and Sparta in two days! Sparta sent back troops, and together with Athens, they defeated Persia.

The last battle of that war was fought in a huge field covered with an herb we call fennel. In Greek, the word for fennel is *marathon*. The battle came to be known in English-language history books as the Battle of Marathon.

Now, in 1896, it looked as if there would be no Olympic trials in the United States that year, because many people had lost interest in the Games, and they thought they were all too expensive. In order to stir up more interest in the Games someone thought of including a twenty-six-mile footrace as one of the events. In memory of the heroic run of Pheidippides and the victorious battle which resulted from it, the race was called a marathon.

The marathon was such a success at the Olympics that the word came to mean any long test of a person's endurance and strength. So marathon refers to other things besides races.

Marmalade

Definition: Marmalade is a kind of jam usually made of oranges. One story says the word comes from a phrase in French. Most experts believe, however, that it developed from Greek and Latin into French, and English borrowed the French word.

In the sixteenth century, Scotland was ruled by Mary Stuart, who is known as Mary, Queen of Scots. She was a good queen, apparently, and her people loved her, but she came to a tragic end. Because she wanted to rule England as well as Scotland, Queen Elizabeth I of England had Mary Stuart beheaded.

Mary is also remembered as a lady who frequently fell into fits of the sulks. She would complain of headache or stomach ache and refuse to eat. The only thing she would accept at these times was a sweet made of honey and oranges.

Now, although Mary was queen of Scotland, the language of her court was French, and most of her servants were from France. When she was in one of her moods the worried servants would scurry around whispering, *Marie est malade,* which meant, "Mary is ill." And they would quickly prepare her favorite honey and oranges. *Marie est malade,* as the story goes, became *Marie malade* and the sweet dish itself came to be known by that name, which was later shortened to *mar-malade.*

A pretty story, perhaps, but not true. Marmalade comes to us, as so many words do, by way of a long voyage from Greek to Latin to Portuguese to French. In Greek, *melimelon* means honey apple. The Romans borrowed this and changed it to *melemelum* to mean sweet apple. The Portuguese form of the word was *marmelo,* which the French turned into marmalade. The English borrowed that word from the French and used it to mean a jam made of oranges.

Robe

Definition: A robe is a long, loose outer garment. Some robes are worn as a sign of important office. Priests, judges and professors wear robes, showing their office or profession. Other robes are the warm, comfortable things we wear around the house or at the beach, such as bathrobes and beachrobes. The word is borrowed from the French.

The overcoat was not invented until the nineteenth century. Before that, people wore long cloaks or capes to keep warm. Pockets are also a recent invention. In the Middle Ages, men carried their money in pouches attached to their belts. The money was then hidden under their cloaks and hard for robbers to get at.

There can never be enough said about how very, very poor most people were in that time. Not only did they have barely enough to eat, they had very few clothes and went about in the worst of weather barefoot and in rags. Robbing the rich was the only way many people could stay alive. The roads were filled with robbers lying in wait for the rich to ride by. Robbers on the road were called highwaymen or footpads.

The best way to get at a rich man's purse, the footpads found, was to sneak up behind him, flip his cloak over his head, grab him around the neck, snatch his purse from his belt and run like a rabbit. By the time the man untangled himself from his thick, long cloak, the robber would be long gone. Usually this worked quite well, but not always. Sometimes, the victim was quick enough to wriggle out of his cloak and escape with his money, leaving his empty cloak in the hands of the unlucky footpad. However, the cloak was considered almost as valuable as gold, because it was so sorely needed for warmth.

The French began to call stolen cloaks *robes*. *Robe* in Old French meant "something stolen." The English borrowed the word and soon used it to mean any cloak or long outer garment.

Sabotage

Definition: Sabotage means to weaken an enemy by secretly destroying its equipment or making it difficult for the enemy to carry out its plans. The word is borrowed from French.

During the Middle Ages most of Europe was divided into feudal estates, and there were but two classes of people—the upper class and the lower class. The upper class, the kings and lords, did little else but make war on their neighbors, hunt wild animals and hold two-month-long houseparties. The lower class, the peasants and the artisans, did nothing else but provide food, clothing, houses and weapons for the upper class so that they could continue their activities.

Peasants and artisans worked from sunup to sundown providing a comfortable life for the kings and lords. Although it is true that in return the lords provided their peasants and artisans with protection against enemies and criminals, it was still an unfair arrangement. Peasants worked eighteen hours a day growing crops and raising animals on their own land or land they rented from the lords. But in return for the protection of the lords, they were made to give up all of their produce, save for just barely enough to keep them alive. It was an exhausting and fairly pointless existence.

French peasants wore heavy, wooden, sharp-heeled shoes called *sabots*. Every once in a while, at harvest time, discouraged, weary and enraged peasants would sneak out at night and stomp down all their crops. The sharp, heavy heels of the sabots ground the crops so deep into the ground that no harvest was possible that season. When the lord came galloping out to the fields demanding his share, all he saw, of course, was broken stalks, crushed fruit and tattered roots. In response to his surprised and angry questions, the peasants would merely shrug and keep silent. The lords would go hungry too.

Eventually, the lords must have realized what was happening to the crops. Either they had spies, or they could tell by the marks of the *sabots* in the ground. In any case, this mysterious destruction of crops came to be known as *sabotage,* which means "something done by a shoe."

By the twentieth century the word had become a common English word meaning any kind of secret damage done to the enemy.

Thug

Definition: A thug is a gangster, often a hired killer. The word comes from Sanskrit.

In India during the thirteenth century, there was a group of religious fanatics who behaved like the assassins of the Old

Man of the Mountain in Persia. The Indian assassins specialized in murder by strangling. To them this widespread murder was a religious duty, and they were never sorry for their awful deeds. They firmly believed they would be blessed by Kah, the Indian goddess of destruction. After strangling their victims they took all their money, and generally became very wealthy. Because of their wealth, and perhaps because of the sneaky ways they lured their victims to their death, a strangler came to be known as a *thag,* which in Sanskrit means "cheat." India was terrorized by the *thags* for six hundred years.

In the nineteenth century, when England made India part of its empire, the English pronounced *thag* as thug, and quickly set about getting rid of them. Those they did not hang they sent out of the country or threw into prison for life. One thag, or thug, confessed to having strangled 931 persons.

The thag organization is long gone. Only our word for them, thug, remains. It is used to mean any gangster or hired killer.

12

INVENTED WORDS

Bangs

Definition: Bangs are front hair which is cut short and worn falling over the forehead. The word comes from a nineteenth-century custom of stable boys who took care of horses.

Hair stylists get their ideas from almost anything. In the eighteenth century, women wore wigs which were sometimes three feet high. Perched on top of that mountain of hair would be a full-rigged miniature ship, or a decorated Christmas tree, or a full-size bird's nest, complete with eggs. About thirty years ago, women wore their hair cut short and tightly curled like a dog's fur. This was called a "poodle cut." Men at that time wore their hair long enough on the sides so that it could be brushed back, with each side meeting at the base of the skull. From the back, a man's head looked like the rear end of a duck, and the style was called a "ducktail cut." There are pony tails, pigtails, corkscrew curls, feather cuts, top knots and French rolls—all hairstyles named for something they try to look like.

The idea for bangs came from the cut of a horse's tail.

Grooming a race horse can take hours. Not only is it necessary to comb and brush the coat until it is sleek, the mane and tail must be combed free of snags and arranged in various ways. Often the mane and tail were braided with ribbons, or the tail done up in a knot. The reason was that a horse runs faster if its tail is kept up out of the mud.

Stable boys did not always have enough time for all this grooming. To save time, they merely whacked off the end of a horse's tail, leaving it cut square at the end. This practice was called "banging off" the tail, and horses with their tails cut like this were called "bangtails." Many bangtails became champion racers. In honor of these square-tailed steeds, hair stylists invented *bangs*.

Bazooka

Definition: A bazooka is a weapon invented during World War II. It is like a portable cannon. It can be carried on the shoulders and has a wide barrel from which small rockets are fired. The rockets have the force to penetrate heavy armored vehicles like tanks. The word was invented by a radio comedian.

When he was young, the radio comedian Bob Burns played in a jazz band. The band rehearsed in the back of a plumbing shop, where there was all kinds of junk lying around. One day, when he had nothing special to do during a rehearsal, he picked up a piece of gas pipe and blew through it. He was delighted by the funny sound it made. The sound was somewhat like that of a mildly worried cow. Then he rolled up a piece of sheet music and put it inside the pipe. When he moved the rolled paper in and out and blew at the same time, he got a variety of notes and could almost play a tune. The thing was getting sillier and sillier, and Burns set about making it sillier still.

He replaced the rolled up paper with a small tin tube. To

this he attached a handle so that the tin tube could be slid in and out of the pipe. Finally, he attached a funnel to the end of the tin tube, and to that he fastened a wire so that he could stretch the tin tube farther out front. The whole thing looked and sounded like a trombone gone crazy. Now it needed a name.

Bob Burns was from Arkansas, and many of the jokes and stories he told on his radio show were based on old sayings of Arkansas people. In Arkansas, when a person talked too much, made little sense, or was too "windy," people said "he blew his bazoo." Bob Burns' instrument was windy, and certainly made little sense. So he called it a bazoo. Then, in order to make the name sound more like a musical instrument, such as a harmonica, he added the "ka," making it bazooka. For years, radio listeners heard the silly sounds of Bob Burns' bazooka, and the instrument was famous all over the United States.

During World War II, the United States army invented a portable rocket-firing weapon to use against enemy tanks. At the time it was being demonstrated it had no name, as far as we know. The story goes that one of the officers watching a demonstration of the new weapon said, "Say, that looks just like Bob Burns' bazooka," and bazooka it became forever after.

Hobby/Hobby Horse

Definitions: A hobby is an enjoyable activity you do in your spare time, like building model airplanes, doing embroidery or playing tennis. A hobby horse is a child's toy, a wooden horse on rockers. Both words come from the English of the fifteenth and sixteenth centuries.

People in the fifteenth and sixteenth centuries loved to watch plays about events in history. Among the most popular were plays about the Moslem, or Moorish, invasions of Europe seven hundred years before. Any play about the Moorish invasions had to have a horse in it, because the Moors were great horsemen. As a matter of fact, it was the Moors who brought the horse to Europe.

Because it was difficult to get a horse onto the stage, the part of the horse had to be played by a man. His costume was a horse made of wicker or straw with a hole cut into its back. The actor

wriggled into the hole and fastened the wicker horse to his waist. Then he pranced and galloped about the stage, showing his version of a fierce Moorish attack. It was the custom in England to nickname all horses Dobbin, Robin, or Hobbin, just as we often nickname all cats Tabby. The horse character of the plays came to be known as "hobbin," then "hobby."

When the wooden rocking horse was invented as a toy for children it was named hobby horse, after the Moorish horse of the plays. The toy was so popular and children loved it so much, people began to call any activity done just for the fun of it a "hobby."

Phony

Definition: Phony in American and English slang means false or pretended. No one knows exactly when the word was first coined. Forms of it were used hundreds of years ago in Ireland and England. The word was brought to America and no longer used in England until American reporters brought it back there during World War II. The dictionary says the origin of the word is unknown. It is probably one of those mysterious invented words.

Here are some theories on the source of phony: It is a short form of "funny business." It comes from "telephone." It comes from Forney, the name of a man who sold cheap fake jewelry in the early days of America. There is little proof for any of these theories.

The linguist Eric Partridge believes the word began with the Irish *fainne,* which means "finger ring." In the eighteenth century, he says, the British underworld, that is, the gangsters and robbers, turned the Irish word into their own slang for someone who passed off gold-painted rings as real gold. Such a person was called a "fawny cove." "Cove" in British slang means man, guy.

"Fawny cove" disappeared from English slang, but turned up in America as "phony man," one who sold cheap, imitation jewelry.

In 1939, as World War II was beginning in Europe, there was some fighting here and there, but no one could be sure whether it would lead to a real war. A Frenchman by the name of Edouard Daladier made a speech about this situation to the French government. In that speech he called the fighting *une drole de guerre.* The phrase could be translated into English as "a joke of a war." But for some reason Americans translated it as "phony war" and American reporters used "phony war" over and over again as they wrote about the events in Europe at that time. Ever since, in history books, the period between 1939 and 1940, just before real war broke out, has been known as the "phony war."

Today, phony is used both in England and America to mean anything which is not what it appears or pretends to be.

13

PEOPLE AND PLACE NAMES
. . .

Bedlam

Definition: Bedlam is a scene of great noise and confusion. The word is a mispronunciation of Bethlehem.

Back around 1200, when this story begins, daily life in Europe was harsh and dangerous. There was very little law and order as we know it today, and certainly no public aid to the poor and sick. Robbers and murderers roamed the countryside at will, and lurked in the dark alleys of towns to prey upon the innocent, the crippled, the poor and sick. To travel a mere ten miles—especially at night—was perilous indeed.

What little control there was came from the Roman Catholic Church. Convents and monasteries were established throughout the countryside and in the towns. They took in travelers for the night and gave them bed and breakfast. At first, this was the only service these establishments provided for strangers. Later, they also became places to house the crippled and sick. Later still, some convents and monasteries became asylums for the insane.

One such place in London was called the Hospital of St. Mary of Bethlehem. It began as a convent which housed and entertained high church officials. The original meaning of hospital, by the way, was "hotel." Early on, the name of the place was shortened to just Bethlehem. Bethlehem became Bethlem, and then Bedlam.

Around 1537, King Henry VIII broke with the Roman Catholic Church and created a new church, the Church of England. He closed most of the monasteries and convents and got rid of the monks and nuns who ran them. Bedlam was taken over by the city of London to be used as a place to lock up the insane. Soon, the word bedlam was used for any institution which housed lunatics.

In those days anyone who was raving mad—or even just a bit weird in some way—was considered possessed by the devil, and he or she was quickly locked up in a bedlam. Not only were these poor creatures locked behind bars, they were chained to walls, beaten regularly, fed only slop and left to sleep in rags on cold, slimy stone floors. As you can imagine, such treatment only worsened their condition. The more they cried and screamed, the more they were beaten; the more they were beaten the louder they howled.

From time to time bedlams were opened to the public. For a small admission fee townspeople could come in and stare at the inmates, just as people today pay to look at animals in a zoo. Sometimes the spectators behaved as wildly as the people they were staring at. As they crowded into the long damp halls of the place, they jostled each other rudely to get a better look. They elbowed and pushed and pointed, giggled and screeched and hollered until it was difficult to tell who were the spectators and who were inmates. The noise, especially on visiting days, could be heard for miles around. It is no wonder then, that bedlam came to mean what it means today: great noise and confusion.

Canter

Definition: A canter is the slow, rocking gait of a horse—faster than a trot, but slower than a gallop. The word comes from the name of the English city, Canterbury.

The highest offices of the English church are in the city of Canterbury. During the twelfth century Henry II was king of England. A man named Thomas à Becket was the head of the English church and was called the Archbishop of Canterbury. As young men, Thomas and Henry were close friends. As they

grew older, when Henry became king and Thomas became archbishop, they became enemies. Henry thought Thomas interfered too much with the government of England, and Thomas thought Henry interfered too much with the church.

Some say Henry thought that Thomas was so dangerous that he had him assassinated. Others argue with that. They say that Thomas's death was the result of a terrible misunderstand-

85

ing. The story goes that one day Henry was so angry with Thomas, he shouted, at no one in particular, "Will someone get rid of that man?" Overhearing his words, some of Henry's men ran out without waiting for orders, and on their own, murdered Thomas inside Canterbury Cathedral.

Very religious people considered the place where Thomas was murdered a shrine, a holy place, and every spring thereafter, pilgrims would come from all over England to pray at the Cathedral of Canterbury. Chaucer's *Canterbury Tales* is about these pilgrims.

Although the pilgrimage was supposed to be a serious religious journey, many people considered it a fine excuse for a relaxing vacation. Canterbury pilgrims were usually a jolly lot, taking in the sights and enjoying the mild spring weather. They never seemed in a great hurry to get to Canterbury. They sang and told stories along the way, and generally enjoyed themselves throughout the whole trip.

Many made the whole journey on foot, but those who could afford it rode horses. As townspeople watched the pilgrims go by every year, they began to call their slow, leisurely pace the "Canterbury gallop," or "Canterbury trot." This was shortened to the "Canterbury," describing the slow, rocking gait of the horses, and shortened again to canter, which is the word we use to this day.

Chauvinist

Definition: A chauvinist is one who thinks his or her country is superior, and all other countries are inferior. ("Male chauvinist" is a term for a man who seems to consider men superior to women.) Chauvinist comes from the name of a French soldier of the eighteenth century, Nicholas Chauvin.

After the long and bloody French Revolution of the eighteenth century, France was in such a dreadful state of disorganization that it took a strong leader to pull it back together again. Napoleon was that leader. Not only did he reorganize France, he proceeded to conquer all of Europe and build an empire. This was the period in history known as the Napoleonic Wars.

Nicholas Chauvin was one of Napoleon's soldiers. It is said he was severely wounded seventeen times in the Napoleonic Wars. For his pains he received a red ribbon and a pension of forty dollars a year. Modern military veterans would hardly be thrilled by these rewards, but Chauvin was proud and grateful to the point of the ridiculous. He spent the rest of his life hobbling around town boring people to tears with his endless tales of the greatness of Napoleon and the glory of the French Empire.

Since Napoleon was eventually roundly defeated and Chauvin had been nearly killed on seventeen separate occasions, most Frenchmen thought Chauvin very silly to be so patriotic. Ever after, a chauvinist was one who made himself ridiculous by wildly overstating the virtues of his country.

These days, some women think some men believe in the superiority of the male sex. They think these men are chauvinists about manhood, and call them "male chauvinists," or— more insultingly—"male chauvinist pigs."

Guy

Definition: Guy is the slang English word for person, fellow or pal. It was the first name of a seventeenth-century Englishman called Guy Fawkes.

Please to remember the fifth of November:
Gunpowder, treason and plot.

This is an old rhyme written in England more than three hundred years ago. It has to do with a plot to blow up the English Parliament on November 5, 1605. Parliament is the law-making body of the English government, something like the United States Congress. The man who plotted the blow-up was named Guy Fawkes.

He and several other men planned to sneak into the houses of Parliament and spread gunpowder on the floor. The gunpowder was to be covered with sticks, so that when a match was lit, the powder would burn slowly enough to allow Guy to get out before the whole building exploded. It was a clever plan, and it very likely would have worked—except for one thing. One of Guy's partners remembered at the last minute that a dear friend of his would be in the building at the time, and he wrote him a note to warn him to get out. On receiving the note, the friend began an investigation. Guy Fawkes was discovered on November 4, arrested, and a year later he was hanged for treason.

Every year thereafter, November 5 in England was known as Guy Fawkes Day. The high point of the celebration is the burning of Guy Fawkes in effigy. Burning in effigy means burning a dummy of the person. Guy Fawkes's dummy is always dressed in dirty ragged clothes. Some years after the first Guy Fawkes Day celebration, anyone dressed in tattered and shabby clothes came to be known as a "guy." Gradually, guy became a short, convenient word meaning any person.

Children in England celebrate Guy Fawkes Day in a way very like the American custom of "trick or treat" on Halloween. On November 5 each year, children make effigies dressed in ragged clothes and go around knocking on doors to ask for "a penny for the Guy."

Lynch

Definition: To lynch is to hang a person illegally. A lynching occurs when people decide to take the law into their own hands. That is, they do not bother with a legal court trial of a suspect, but simply decide on short notice and with little evidence that the suspect is guilty, and hang the person then and there. The word comes from the name of an eighteenth-century American, Colonel William Lynch.

We have all seen movie westerns in which the posse charges out after cattle rustlers, catches them, accuses them and hangs them from the nearest and most convenient tree—all in the space of an hour or two. This procedure occurred frequently in the United States in areas where there was no organized law and order. If there was a great deal of crime in an area and the courts of law too difficult to get to, citizens tried to keep order and deal with criminals in their own way. This might have been efficient and time-saving, but it was unjust and illegal, for our laws say that every person has the right to a trial by jury in court, no matter what the accusation, and until proven guilty the person has to be considered innocent. Unfortunately, many people in our history have disobeyed that law. One such person was Colonel William Lynch.

Shortly after the American Revolution, Lynch formed a citizens' association of law enforcers. He claimed that crime was so widespread and local law enforcement so inadequate that the citizens had to clean up their county in their own way. Colonel Lynch himself was often both judge and jury for suspects of crimes.

A great deal of what we know about Colonel Lynch comes from the opinions in the diary of one Andrew Ellicot. Ellicot visited Lynch in 1811 and wrote down their conversation. He assured his readers that all he had written was exactly as Lynch told it to him. Lynch's special brand of legal procedure came to be known as "lynch laws," and they worked like this:

Someone would come to the Lynch citizens' association accusing a person of a crime. The association would then immediately set out after the accused, capture him and hold him for questioning. Ellicot tells us that if the accused did not at first give the answers the association wanted, he was whipped until he did. Then, as Ellicot wrote:

> The person . . . was placed on a horse with his hands tied behind him and a rope around his neck which was fastened to the limb of a tree over his head. In this situation the person was left, and when the horse in pursuit of food or any other cause moved from his position the unfortunate person was left suspended by the neck.

Now, Lynch denied that he ever actually sentenced a person to death. However, he did admit that sometimes hangings "happened." This was because, you see, the accused "happened" to be sitting on a horse under a tree while he was being tried. There "happened" to be a rope around his neck, and the rope "happened" to be tied to the branch of the tree. If the horse "happened" to bolt out from under the tree—well, the rest you can imagine for yourself.

Lynch called these "happened" hangings "aiding the civil authorities." We call them lynching.

Sandwich

Definition: A sandwich is two pieces of bread with some filling between them. The word comes from the name of an eighteenth-century Englishman, John Montague, the fourth Earl of Sandwich.

During the time of the American Revolution, John Montague, the fourth Earl of Sandwich, was first lord of the Admiralty, the highest office in the British Navy. The Hawaiian Islands were originally named the Sandwich Islands in his honor, not because anyone thought he was honorable, but because he happened to be first lord of the Admiralty at the time they were discovered.

Actually, he was extremely unpopular in England. His public life was one of dishonesty and inefficiency, and his pri-

vate life was full of scandal. At one time, for example, he belonged to an association called the Hell Fire Club, which was rumored to hold black masses, worship the devil and do all kinds of nasty things.

Montague, among other things, was an incurable gambler, and often spent the whole night at the gaming tables. One night, as the story goes, he was so involved at cards, he did not want to leave the table long enough to eat a full meal. Dinners at that time were lengthy affairs, sometimes lasting six hours or more. So, he ordered a servant to bring him two pieces of bread with a slice of meat between them. Thereafter, whenever he was in a gambling mood, he did the same thing.

It is likely that the busy servant soon tired of telling the cook every night, "Two pieces of bread with a slice of meat between them for the fourth Earl of Sandwich." He must have soon shortened the order to a hurried, "Fix a sandwich." From then on, whenever two pieces of bread were divided by some kind of filling, the result was called a sandwich.

Sequoia

Definition: Sequoia is the name of the giant redwood tree of California. One of these trees is so large it spans a two-lane highway, and a tunnel has been carved into it allowing cars to pass through. The tree is named after a Cherokee Indian.

In Part I of this book we said that American Indian languages had no written form. If we are to believe either of the stories below, we have to say that is not exactly true. There is a Cherokee alphabet, but just who invented it, and when, remains a mystery.

Dictionaries tell us Sequoia was the name of a Cherokee scholar. Most books on words tell us Sequoia was a brilliant Cherokee Indian who accomplished something no other Indian or European had been able to do—put the Cherokee language into a written form.

According to one story, Sequoia had been an excellent hunter until a hunting accident broke his leg. The leg never healed properly, and he was never able to hunt again. Having much time on his hands, he set about studying the ways of the white people, especially their language. He was fascinated by the whites' ability to read and write, and he realized these abilities gave people power. He called the papers whites read from "talking leaves," and he felt the Cherokee nation would be greatly advanced if it had "talking leaves" of its own.

Every day, the story continues, he went off by himself into the woods, and for ten years he labored to produce a Cherokee alphabet. As he limped around, muttering to himself and making odd scratches on tree bark, his friends and family thought he was either doing black magic or going mad. They left him strictly alone. At the end of ten years, we are told, he came out of the woods with an alphabet of eighty-six characters, or letters.

Not only did the alphabet represent every sound in the Cherokee language, it was so simple anyone could learn to read it in a single day. Sequoia first taught it to one of his daughters. Then the two of them went to the tribal chief to demonstrate their new talking leaves. The chief was impressed and gave Sequoia and his daughter permission to teach it to all the other Cherokees.

Whites were so impressed by Sequoia's brilliant accomplishment they named the beautiful giant California redwood tree in his honor.

"Not true!" says a man named Traveller Bird. According to Traveller Bird, who claims to be a direct descendant of the real Sequoia, that story is packed with misunderstanding, misinformation and outright lies. In a book called *Tell Them They Lied,* he tells his version of the story.

In the first place, the man the whites claimed to be Sequoia—an Indian given the English name George Guess—was not Sequoia. For that matter, Traveller Bird tells us, Sequoia probably never existed at all, and the man associated with the Cherokee alphabet was actually a man named Sogwili, Traveller Bird's ancestor.

In the second place, neither Sequoia, nor George Guess, nor Sogwili just "suddenly" invented an alphabet in the nineteenth century. The Cherokee alphabet had been read and written since the fifteenth century.

The story, according to Traveller Bird, is this: The Cherokee nation had long been divided into clans and societies, each with its own specialization. Sogwili was a member of the seven-clan Scribe Society. These scribes, or writers, had the responsibility of teaching the alphabet to all the other clans. Sogwili was not the inventor of the alphabet; he was a teacher. He and other members of his clan taught their people not only Cherokee but also Latin and other European languages they learned from missionaries.

But the knowledge was kept secret from the white people, and what is known as the Cherokee alphabet was actually a secret code. According to Traveller Bird, the whites were afraid to allow the Indians to be highly educated, fearing that once they were, they would rise up against the settlers. So, rather than honor the Cherokees for their ability to read and write, they murdered them. Sogwili's Scribe Society was destroyed, nearly to the last man.

As one of the few survivors, Sogwili continued to teach his people in secret. When the whites found him out and discovered the secret code, they wanted to hang him, and they nearly did. But at the last minute they changed their minds. Most white Americans realized this was going too far, and it would look bad to the rest of the world. In order to hide the fact they had been outsmarted by the Cherokees, and in order to make it look as if relations with the Indians were peaceful, they made up the story of Sequoia and his "invention" of a Cherokee alphabet. They chose George Guess, whose Indian name sounded to them like Sequoia, as the "inventor," because he was a harmless little man who had long been friendly with the whites.

Today, Traveller Bird tells us, thirteen thousand full-blooded Cherokees living in eastern Oklahoma, the Smoky Mountains of North Carolina and in parts of Mexico still speak

94

and read their own language and still write in the secret Cherokee code.

Which story are we to believe? Here is a fine mystery for word detectives to investigate further.

Spoonerism

Definition: A spoonerism is the mispronunciation of the beginning sounds of two or more words said one after the other. For example, the sentence, "Chirping birds perched on a branch" could be mispronounced as a spoonerism that would sound like this: "Burping cherds berched on a panch." The word comes from the name of a nineteenth-century minister and history professor, the Reverend William A. Spooner.

Most of us become very nervous if we have to speak before an audience, and we often mispronounce our words. Or, when we are in a hurry to say something we mix the whole thing up by transposing, or switching, the initial sounds. The results are hilarious, and very, very embarassing.

This kind of error is called a spoonerism after the Reverend William A. Spooner, who lived in Oxford, England during the nineteenth century. He made this kind of slip of the tongue all the time. When he wanted to talk about a "half-formed wish," it came out "half-warmed fish." Wanting to refer to "our dear old queen," he said instead "our queer old dean." In one of his sermons he wanted to say, "Our Lord is a loving shepherd," but shocked the congregation by roaring, "Our Lord is a shoving leopard!"

Do you get the idea? If so, then you can figure out for yourself what the poor Reverend had in mind when he demanded angrily of a student, "Why did you hiss my mystery lecture?" He expelled another student during the school year because the student had been very lazy, and, as the Reverend put it, "had tasted two worms."

14

OLD WORDS

Abacus/Calculate/Calculator/ Calculus

Definitions: An abacus is a device for counting. It is a rectangular frame with wires or rods attached top and bottom. Counting is done by pushing the beads up and down the wires. The word comes from Greek. To calculate is to count or figure mathematically. A calculator is a machine for counting. Calculus is a branch of mathematics. The words come from Latin.

Today, students, businessmen, engineers, and housewives carry little electronic calculators with them everywhere. People of the twentieth century are not the first ones to use machines to help them do their mathematics. The ancient Romans had a calculator they called an *abacus,* a word they borrowed from the Greek *abax.* The abacus we know today is the device described above, and the only place we are likely to see one is in a toy store. They are made for children to help them learn to count. The only place they are actually used for calculation is in some parts of Asia. What the Romans called an *abacus* was not a device made up of a frame and wires. Their *abacus* was a board partitioned off into narrow channels. Romans counted by putting

pebbles into the channels and pushing them backward and forward. The Latin word for pebble was *calculus*. From that word we get calculus, the branch of mathematics, and calculate, to count or figure.

Applaud/Explode

Definitions: Applaud means to clap in approval of a performance. Explode means to split apart with a great noise. Both words have to do with the ancient Greek theater, and they come to us by way of Latin.

The theater of the western world was invented nearly three thousand years ago by the ancient Greeks. Later, it was borrowed by the Romans when they made Greece part of their empire.

As they are today, Greek plays were held in the open air in amphitheaters, which looked something like football stadiums. Imagine a giant natural bowl with rows of long ridges cut into its sides for seats. At the bottom of the bowl, at one end of the oval was a round platform called the orchestra, which was the stage. Amphitheaters could seat as many as thirty thousand people, and everybody came to see the plays. It was standing room only.

The same plays were performed over and over again, and everyone soon knew the stories by heart. But the people did not come to see how a story turned out; they already knew. They came to see how well the plays were acted. Everybody was a

critic, and usually the audience was very loud with their opinions on the actors' art. So loud, in fact, that soldiers had to be posted here and there to keep order. They carried long staffs which they used to rap the heads of unruly members of the audience.

Imagine the din at a Super Bowl football game and you can imagine what a noisy affair a Greek play could be. Just before the play began, as the actors came out on the stage, it was the custom to clap in welcome and approval. From then on, if the actors were doing well, the audience watched fairly quietly. Occasionally, an enthusiastic spectator might get so involved in the play he would shout out to the actors or recite along with them. But he was always quickly silenced by the soldiers' staffs. In general, as long as the actors were good, the audience watched with great interest, enjoyment and respect.

But woe to the actor who did not know his art! If he forgot his lines, or stumbled, or did not show the right emotion, the audience would clap again — not in approval this time, but in anger and disgust. Thirty thousand people would keep on clapping, steadily, until the actor's voice was drowned out and he was driven from the stage by the deafening roar of disapproval.

In Latin, to clap hands in approval at the beginning of a play is *applaudere,* from which we get applaud and applause. The Latin *explaudere* meant "to clap someone off the stage." From *explaudere* we get explode and explosion. The sudden thundering noise made by an angry audience is probably what gave us the modern meaning of explosion.

If explosion is a word related to both a loud noise and an angry audience, what a strange coincidence that in today's slang an unsuccessful show is known as a "bomb"!

Ballot/Blackball

Definitions: A ballot is a piece of paper on which we write our vote. Blackball means to refuse to allow someone to become a member of a club or society. Ballot comes to us from Latin, but the custom of voting began with the ancient Greeks.

Many of our modern democratic ideas of law and government began with the ancient Romans and Greeks. But their governments were not as democratic as ours. Although they had the custom of voting, they did not allow everyone to vote. They kept slaves, and of course slaves couldn't vote. Nor could women, or people who did not own property, or people who were citizens but not native born. Of those who were allowed to vote, many could not read or write. So, instead of writing their votes, they used other means.

Ballot comes from the Latin *ballotta,* which means "little ball." It was the Roman custom to vote by dropping little white or black balls into a container—white for yes and black for no. Today, certain clubs and secret societies still use this method of voting on whether or not a person should be allowed into the club or thrown out of it. If you hear that a person has been "blackballed" from a group it means he or she has been denied membership or has been forced out, having received more black balls than white balls. The expression probably comes from the Roman method of voting.

The ancient Greeks voted in a similar way, but they used other objects as well as balls—shells, colored pebbles, bits of metal, or even beans. Apparently beans were used quite frequently as ballots, because politicians were called "bean eaters."

Berserk

Definition: Berserk means a state of violent or destructive rage. The expression "to go berserk" means to go suddenly wild and insane, destroying property and injuring, sometimes even killing, people. The word comes from an old Norse word in the language of the Vikings.

"From the fury of the Northmen Lord deliver us!" So goes a ninth-century Anglo-Saxon prayer. Whoever composed that prayer must have had in mind a certain legendary Viking war-

100

rior who is supposed to have gone into battle in such a crazy rage he could destroy most of the enemy single handed. From the legends we can imagine a giant of a man, well over six feet tall, with shoulders and chest as broad as a bull. He probably had long yellow hair and a spiky beard the color of corn husks. His eyes were the icy blue of the cold mountain lakes of his homeland.

Viking soldiers carried shields to protect themselves and wore an armor called chain mail. This was a shirt of interlocking metal rings riveted together. Their helmets were made of iron, with a rounded crown which fit over the skull. To the crown was attached a metal plate which covered the upper part of the face. Two slits were cut out for the eyes, leaving a rectangle between to protect the nose. The helmet looked very much like the upper part of a modern ski mask, and gave the wearer a weird and menacing look.

The Viking weapon was a deadly, heavy sword with cutting edges on either side and handles carved in precious metals. These swords were so heavy that even our legendary Viking needed two hands to swing it. However, he wore no helmet, carried no shield and wore no more for protection than a shirt made from the skin of a bear. The shirt was called a *beresht*.

He was either terribly brave or totally mad. At any rate, in his frenzy to conquer he must have thought he could not be killed. His fame spread far and wide as that wild killer in a bearskin shirt. Eventually he and his twelve sons took *beresht* as their family name. In Anglo-Saxon *beresht* became berserk, and many Norse conquerors came to be known as berserkers.

Of course, not all Vikings were berserkers. History tells us many were basically peaceful. They were brave explorers, clever traders, good farmers and excellent craftsmen and ship-builders. After the bloodshed of the Viking conquest, England benefited greatly from the language and law and customs of these invaders. But the "fury of the Northmen" is not to be forgotten. It is remembered every time a disturbed person races his or her car through a crowd of pedestrians or someone goes into a rage and begins to shoot at innocent people. When these things happen, we say the person has "gone berserk."

Blackmail

Definition: To blackmail someone is to demand money or special favors for promising to protect them or keep their secrets. Money paid for this purpose is also known as "protection money" or "hush money." The word comes from a custom in Scotland during the Middle Ages. At that time, it had nothing to do with the color black or with mail (letters) as we use those words today.

Throughout Europe and the British Isles during the Middle Ages most people were poor. Only the ruling classes were rich. Honest folk made a modest living as farmers or craftsmen. Although some of these became somewhat prosperous, they were never really wealthy. Out of their small earnings, farmers had to pay taxes to the church and to their rulers. Sometimes taxes were paid in money, but since most farmers rarely had any, most payments were made in crops or livestock. Payment of any kind was known as *mail.*

Since farming was a poor business to begin with, and farmers were made poorer by the taxes they had to pay, many farmers decided the best way to get rich and avoid taxes was to turn to robbery. For many years, the territory along the border between England and Scotland was under the control of roving bands of robbers on horseback. They galloped through the fields, burning crops, burglarizing houses and stealing sheep and cattle and horses. They patrolled the roads, attacking wealthy travelers to rob them of their gold and silver.

The robbers were constantly on the move. They rarely stayed in one place, for fear of being caught. Certainly, they did no farming. They needed a steady supply of food for themselves and their horses. It was not always safe for them to use the gold and silver they stole from travelers to buy supplies. So they demanded that farmers set aside crops and livestock to pay the robbers. If the farmers did not do this, the robbers would steal everything anyway. What choice did the farmers have? They paid. Sometimes, they paid in silver, if they had any, and this was called "white mail." Payment in crops and livestock, the more usual payment, was called "black mail," and that is the word we use today for payment which is forced out of someone by threats to do them harm.

Bonfire

Definition: A bonfire is any large fire built in the open air. The word comes to us from Anglo-Saxon.

Today, we associate a bonfire with enjoyment and good things, like telling stories around a campfire or roasting marshmallows at the beach. For this reason, it used to be thought that bonfire was originally a French word meaning "good fire." In French *bon* means "good." But this is wrong. The word is from the Anglo-Saxon word for "bone fire," and its meaning is not good at all. Since pagan times, large, outdoor fires have been associated with horror and evil.

In ancient times many peoples would regularly select men and women to be burned to death in great fires at the altars of their gods. They believed this would show they loved their gods more than themselves. The custom is known as human sacrifice. The fires in which the people were sacrificed were the earliest examples of bone fires.

Christianity and other religions eventually outlawed human sacrifice, calling it murder, which it was. But Christians continued to kill people in bone fires for other reasons. During the Middle Ages in Europe death by fire was a common punishment for crime—not only murder and robbery, but many other things as well, things we do not consider crimes at all today.

One of these "crimes" was heresy. Heresy meant no more than forming and expressing an opinion the church did not approve of, and was punishable by death. The person who committed heresy was called a heretic. Many heretics were "burned at the stake." This was a custom as ghastly and brutal as the human sacrifice of pagan times. The convicted heretic was tied high up on a long pole, the stake, which was stuck into the middle of a large fire. The person died in slow agony in flames so hot they burned even the bones.

Then there was the "crime" of witchcraft. In those days, there was very little education and almost no knowledge of science, even among the few who could read and write. Having no natural explanation for misfortunes and disasters, people considered them the work of the devil. The devil had many helpers, they were sure, and these helpers were witches. Witches were blamed for fire, flood, disease, injury, dead livestock, missing children and even for things as unimportant as broken dishes. Anyone who looked a bit odd, or behaved in a strange way, and happened to be around during a disaster could be called a witch and blamed for the trouble. Many innocent people whose only "crime" might have been to be mentally ill, crippled, or merely ugly were burned at the stake along with heretics, many of whom were also considered to be witches. In short, it was a crime to be different, and those who were different could die in a bone fire.

There is another example of bone fires in Europe during the Middle Ages. These were horrible, but they were necessary. Several times, between the twelfth and seventeenth centuries, the population of Europe was nearly wiped out by a terrible disease called the Black Death (bubonic plague). We know now that the disease was carried by rats and spread to humans by fleas. Since there was no sanitation as we know it today, and people rarely bathed, rats outnumbered people and people were covered with fleas. The disease spread with unbelievable speed. Within weeks nearly a whole town could be dead. The disease spread so fast, and there were so few people left alive, it was impossible to bury all the dead. So the few survivors collected the bodies in wagons and burned them all together in gigantic fires outside the towns. These bone fires, horrible as they were, actually did some good, and could be called *bon*fires, or "good fires," because they rid the towns of plague germs, destroyed the fleas and sent the rats scurrying into hiding elsewhere.

Eventually, the bubonic plague disappeared from Europe. People became more educated, sanitation improved and science produced treatment and cures for the disease. As education improved, people became more reasonable. They no longer believed in witches, and heresy was no longer a crime. No one, not even a murderer, was ever again punished by being burned to death. Bone fires became the innocent bonfires we enjoy today.

Chess/Checkmate/Exchequer/ Checkers/Check

Definitions: There are about twelve different variations of the meaning of check in English, and most of them are related in some way to the ancient game of chess. Chess comes from one of the Arabic languages spoken in Persia.

Chess was invented in India nearly two thousand years ago. The Arabs, who traded with the countries of Asia and the Middle East, brought the game to Persia. Then, in the eighth century, when the Arabs controlled the Mediterranean Sea and occupied southern Europe, they brought the game to Spain. From there it spread throughout Europe.

The most important piece in the game is the king. When the king is maneuvered into a place from which he cannot escape, the game is over. The Persian word for king is *shah,* and the word for dead or killed is *mat.* In Arabic and Persian the winning player at the end of the game would say *shah mat,* meaning, "the king is dead." In old Spanish this became *xaque mate* (HAH-kay MA-tay). In old French it was *eschec mat,* and in Middle English, *chek mate.* In modern English this is checkmate, and to warn that the opponent's king is unprotected, we say "Check!"

The French called the game *esches,* which was the plural for *eschec,* and meant king. The English dropped the initial *es* from *esches* making it *ches,* then *chess.* The name of the game really means "kings."

The game called checkers is a simplified form of chess.

The word exchequer comes from the game of chess. It is used more in England than in the United States. The Court of the Exchequer in England is that branch of the government which collects tax money. In both countries exchequer can be used to mean any organization that holds and controls money. A bank can be called an exchequer. This is how the word is related to chess.

In the twelfth century, Europeans were still using Roman numerals instead of the numbers we use today, which are Arabic. Since it is impossible to add and subtract in writing with Roman numerals, city officials in the twelfth century counted and recorded tax money by arranging it on a large table which had been marked off into squares like a chessboard. The group of officials who sat at the squared off table and collected money was known as the *exchequer*, because of the similarity of their counting table to a chessboard. And, if you look at the word carefully, you can see that it looks somewhat like the old French word for king — *eschec*. Today, when you write a check to the bank, you are ordering an exchequer to pay a sum of money. (In England, a bank check is spelled cheque.)

There are at least four other meanings of check which are related to the game of chess. Check can mean to control. You "check your dog" by holding it on a leash. You "check the progress" of a disease by taking medicine. This is the same idea as "checking the king" in chess; you control him by getting him into a place from which he cannot escape easily.

We use the word check to mean making sure something is correct or secure. "Check your spelling test." "Check the doors to see that they are locked." When a chess player says "Check!" he or she is warning the king to be careful.

In the Old West, almost everyone carried guns. In church, at dances or in saloons, men were told to "Check their guns at the door." This was to get the guns out of the way so there would be no trouble. Today, in a restaurant or other public place we can "check our hats and coats" to get them out of the way. In chess, when the king is "checked" he is in a place where he can't cause trouble; he is temporarily out of the way.

Checks, or checked or checkered material is related to chess because it has the pattern of a chessboard.

So, if you put on a checked hat, go to a bank, with your dog on a leash, leave your hat at the door, write a check and look it over to make sure it is correct, remember that all this began with a game played in India nearly two thousand years ago.

Curfew

Definition: A curfew is a certain hour at night at which everyone should be off the streets and at home. The word comes from French.

If your parents tell you to be home by a certain hour at night, you have a curfew. Today, in times of danger or trouble—enemy attack, riots in the streets, or simply a temporary shortage of electric power—a city might declare a curfew, an hour at which everyone should be off the streets and all the lights put out. In times of political crisis a curfew may be declared so that a government can enforce order. At other times, in cases of natural disaster, a curfew might be called for the protection of the citizens.

The word dates back to France of the Middle Ages, and comes from the French *couvre feu,* which means "cover the fire." In Europe during the Middle Ages most houses were one-room wooden dwellings with roofs thatched of dried grass. All heat and light came from a fire built in a hole dug into the middle of the floor. The chimney was no more than a hole in the dried grass roof. All too frequently, sparks and cinders landed on the roof and started fires which could rage through a whole town and destroy it within minutes.

In France, after many of these disasters, city authorities finally made it a law that someone in the town ring a bell at bedtime every night to remind the people to *couvre feu*—cover their fires. When the French conquered England in 1066, they brought the law and the word with them. English people obeyed the law but mispronounced the word, calling that hour of the night curfew.

Debonair

Definition: A debonair person is one who is well-mannered, good natured and light hearted. The word comes from French.

A popular sport in Europe during the Middle Ages was falconry. Falcons, large hawklike birds, were kept as pets and trained to fly off—sometimes for miles—to hunt smaller birds and then return to their masters' hands. The falcon is a large, heavy bird with claws or talons as hard as steel. The falconer must wear a heavy leather glove to protect his hand and arm from being pierced or gashed by the tightly gripping talons. By nature the falcon is a fierce bird. It is a hunter, after all. Some were even bred to have teeth on the ends of their beaks so they could hunt better, and their fierceness was encouraged. But some pet falcons were tame and gentle.

People enjoyed watching these graceful birds soar into the sky and swoop back down. Contests were held to see which birds were the most beautiful and the best hunters. Champions with the sleekest feathers, broadest wingspread, most graceful flight, and gentlest nature were said by the French to be *de bonne aire,* meaning "of good air."

After falconry was no longer such a popular sport, the phrase *de bonne aire* remained in the language to describe a well-mannered person of graceful and elegant appearance. In English, the words of the French phrase were run together to make one word and spelled debonair.

Dismal

Definition: Anything dismal is dark, dull and depressing. There are two theories about the source of the word. One theory is that it comes from the Latin decima, *meaning ten, which became the Old French* disme, *meaning one tenth. The other theory is that it began with the Latin* dies mali *which became Old French* dis mal *meaning bad days.*

During the Middle Ages, when people were not paying robbers blackmail, they were paying high taxes to the church and to their rulers. The percentage of income required by both church and rulers for taxes was one tenth. That means that two tenths, or one fifth, or twenty percent of a poor farmer's money, crops and livestock went for taxes. Then as now, tax time came regularly, and everything had to be paid out at once. In their case the time was harvest time. Then as now, having paid out so much all at once, the people were twenty percent poorer and one hundred percent depressed. In Old French a one-tenth tax was called a *disme*. In Middle English slang a poor, discouraged farmer at tax time was said to be "in the dismal."

Another theory has nothing to do with taxes. It has to do with the old belief that certain days of every month are dangerous, evil days. In the early Middle Ages, calendars were different from the way they are today. The number of days in the year, the number of months, and so on, were calculated on the basis of the mathematics and astronomy of the Egyptians. Now, while the Egyptians were very advanced in these sciences, they were also very superstitious, and Europeans of the Middle Ages were more superstitious still. Early European calendars were marked with what were called "Egyptian days"—the dangerous days— and in Latin they were called *dies mali*. In Old French this became *dis mal*, and in Middle English the two French words were blended to make the word we use today. On *dis mal*, or dismal days, most people believed it was unwise to take any risks at all.

Egyptian calculations to determine the yearly bad days were very exact. The dangerous days were: January 1 and 25; February 4 and 26; March 1 and 28; April 10 and 20; May 3 and 25; June 10 and 16; July 13 and 22; August 1 and 30; September 3 and 21; October 3 and 22; November 5 and 28; December 7 and 22.

Dragon/Dragoon

Definitions: A dragon is a mythical monster with the body of a snake, sometimes with wings, sometimes with several heads. Almost all dragons breathe fire. A dragoon is a member of a branch of the British army. Both words come from ancient Greek.

The *dragon* or *drakon* of the ancient Greeks was a giant serpent with three heads. It was blood red to begin with, but could change its color at will. It spit fire from each of its three heads.

Many other peoples believed in dragons, and their folklore and stories usually featured at least one of these monsters. For the Chinese, the dragon is a symbol of good luck. Chinese New Year parades usually include a giant "human dragon." Several people line up and crouch under a long dragon made of paper painted to look like scales. The head has a large gaping mouth and long slanted fiery eyes. It is brilliantly colored in red, yellow, green and orange.

The Vikings carved dragon heads on the prows of their ships. So firmly did the Vikings believe in the power of dragons that just before landing on the shores of a foreign country they would remove the dragon's head so that it could not communicate with or warn the evil spirits on land.

The patron saint of England is Saint George. He is best known for his strength, cleverness and skill at saving beautiful maidens from dragons. During the Crusades, English soldiers, believing themselves to be as holy and heroic as Saint George, carried banners decorated with pictures of fiery dragons. In England at that time the word was spelled and pronounced dragoon.

While the dragons of different countries all varied somewhat in shape and color, one thing they all seemed to have in common was the ability to breathe fire. When guns were invented they were called dragoons by the English because of the fire which exploded from the barrels. Later, the mounted troops who carried these new firearms were also called dragoons. Early dragoons must have been a fierce and frightening force, for "to dragoon" means to take complete control of the enemy with violence and severe cruelty in an attack more horrifying than any mythical dragon.

Fanatic

Definition: A fanatic is a person so deeply involved with a single subject or cause that he or she cannot think or talk about anything else. Winston Churchill said a fanatic is "one who can't change his mind and won't change the subject." Some fanatics become so violent in their beliefs they kill. The word comes from Latin.

Our word "fan" is a shortened form of fanatic and means something much milder than fanatic. Fans are people who have a keen interest in something. There are baseball fans, mystery fans, rock music fans, and so on. Letters written to entertainment stars are known as fan mail. While the behavior of the crowd at a baseball game or rock concert can get fairly wild, and the contents of fan letters are sometimes quite insane, none of

that comes near the weird and murderous behavior of the true fanatic.

Assassins are often fanatics. People who accused others of witchcraft and had them burned at the stake were fanatics. Throughout history, many leaders have been known as fanatics. The Old Man of the Mountain and his band of "hashishin" were fanatics. During the sixteenth century, England had a queen they called "Bloody Mary," because of the number (around 300) of Protestants who were executed by the government. In the eighteenth century, Cotton Mather, a governor of Massachusetts, stirred up feelings that led to the Salem Witch Trials. During World War II, one of the worst fanatics of all time, Adolf Hitler, had six million Jews put to death in gas chambers.

The word comes from the first century B.C. during the early days of the Roman Empire. A general named Sulla was fighting a battle far away from Rome in Asia Minor. While he was there, he had a dream in which a goddess of war named Bellona came to warn him that back in Rome his enemies were plotting to kill him. She urged him to return immediately.

He did, and found that Bellona had told him the truth. He managed to defeat his enemies, and in gratitude to the goddess he built her a temple. The Latin word for temple is *fane.* A priest of the temple was known as a *fanaticus;* the plural, priests, was *fanatici.*

The religious rites at the *fane* of Bellona were grim and dreadful. The *fanatici* wore black robes which covered them from head to foot. At the height of the religious ceremony they would tear their robes to shreds and gash themselves with double edged axes. Then they splattered blood upon the worshipers. People believed it was either Bellona or the *fane* itself which stirred the priests to such a frenzy. Eventually, anyone who behaved in this violently insane way at a religious rite came to be known as a *fanticus,* and then, in the English version, a fanatic.

Gossip

Definition: Gossip is rumors, tattle tales and idle talk about others behind their backs. The word comes from Old English.

When a baby is baptized and given a name, it is the custom to appoint two persons who are not part of the family to be

115

responsible for the child's spiritual welfare and religious training. These two persons are known as the godparents. The
custom dates back many centuries in Christianity. Since godparents were not blood relations, but persons chosen from
outside the family, and since their job was to watch out for the
child's soul, they were said to be "related in God." The Old
English word for "related in God" was *godsib*. *Sib* meant "related," and you can see that word today in the modern word
sibling, which means "brother" or "sister."

Now, the *godsib* not only had a responsibility to the child,
they took the right to talk among themselves about the child,
about his parents, about his whole family. It is likely their con-
versations often included rumors and idle talk: "Really, Gwendolyn should teach that child better manners." Or, "They say
that Otto beats his wife on rainy Sundays." Or, "Have you
looked under the beds in that house? Gwendolyn should use the
broom more often. That house is no fit place to raise our
godchild. . . ." And so on.

Soon *godsib* came to mean anyone who whispered tattle

tales or spread rumors about people behind their backs. This kind of sneaky talk itself came to be known as *godsib* also. As it so often happens with English words, pronunciation of *godsib* was blurred. Remember how Bethlehem became Bethlem and then Bedlam? In *godsib,* the *d* was dropped and the *b* sound at the end became *p* so that the word gossip developed. As in the case of bedlam, the mispronunciation was spelled the way it sounded, and thus the word came down to us.

Handicap

Definition: A handicap is a disadvantage. A handicapped person is one who has a disability that makes it difficult to perform mentally or physically like other people. In games and sports, a handicap can be either a disadvantage or an advantage. It is something given to or taken away from players in order that all will start with an even chance to win. The word comes from the name of a game played in England in the fourteenth century.

There is some disagreement as to how the game of handicap was played, which is not surprising, since the game has not been played for five hundred years. Basically, it went something like this: Two men would decide to trade articles of clothing—a pair of gloves for a belt, for example. Since these two things were not of equal value, the players chose a third man to act as umpire to decide on the value of each item and state how much extra money should be paid when the trade was made.

All three players then put a certain amount of money called "forfeit money" into a cap. Forfeit money means money to be given up. After the umpire decided on the value of the articles the players would decide whether or not to trade. They would then reach into their pockets and bring out their hands closed in a fist. At a certain signal they would open their hands over the cap. By putting more money into the cap a player would show he wanted to trade. If both put money in, the trade was made, and the umpire took the forfeit money. If neither put in money there was no trade and the umpire again took the forfeit money. If one put in money and the other didn't there was no trade, but the one who did put money in won the forfeit money. All of this putting of coins into a cap came to be known as "hand-in-the-cap," which was shortened to hand-in-cap, and finally handicap.

Later, when horseracing had become a popular sport, umpires were chosen to decide how much weight the horses should carry. The different weights they decided on came to be known as handicaps. The word became a common term used in many sports and games.

Since players of hand-in-the-cap and other gambling games which came after it were taking the risk of losing money, handicap also came to mean any condition which can make things difficult for us.

Idiot

Definition: Idiots are persons whose mental powers are so weak they cannot do anything for themselves. In recent years the term "severely mentally retarded" has replaced idiot to describe such a person, but idiot continues to be used as an insulting word for anyone we think behaves in a stupid or silly way. The original meaning was far different from the modern meaning. The word comes from Greek.

In Greek, the word *idio* means "personal" or "individual." From the word *idio* and the idea of "individual" the ancient Greeks formed the word *idiotes. Idiotes* were private citizens who did not hold public office or serve in the government. Gradually the meaning expanded to include anyone who did not have any specific knowledge of something or any special skill. It did not mean a stupid person; it meant a nonpolitician, or a nondoctor, or a nonteacher. An *idiote* was a person who was perfectly intelligent, but was not a member of any special profession.

When the Romans made Greece part of their empire and began borrowing parts of the Greek language, they often gave their own meanings to Greek words. Romans reasoned that anyone not holding public office, that is, any *idiote,* just might be stupid. A lack of interest in government, they began to believe, was probably a sign of low intelligence—a sign that the person was not smart enough for anything.

In time, *idiotes* entered other languages and the original meanings of nonoffice-holder or nonprofessional were completely lost. The word became idiot in English and came into the language with the meaning of a person so dull, stupid and unskilled he or she could do nothing.

Infantry

Definition: The infantry is the branch of an army which goes into battle on foot. The modern infantry rides trucks and tanks, but it still spends most of its time marching. The word comes from Latin.

An infantryman, or foot soldier, is a tough and rugged individual. He tramps through the mud, freezes in rain and snow, or swelters in the sun. He climbs mountains, crawls through jungles and drags across the desert sands. It would not be wise to tell him his unit is made up of babies, but the Latin word for babies is the original meaning of infantry.

The word comes from *infans,* meaning one who cannot speak. From *infans* came the legal term *infant* meaning one who has not reached the age to speak for himself. *Infant* in Latin and the Romance languages came to mean any child. The word then became a term of affection. Just as in English a mother might call her adult son or daughter "baby," or lovers call each other "baby," so Europeans used a form of *infant* in an affectionate way.

In the army of ancient Rome only the officers rode horses. The rest of the army went on foot. Officers took on young boys as their personal servants. After the boys had done their chores and it was time to go into battle, they marched along with the foot soldiers. In Italian the boy servants came to be known affectionately as the *infanteria*—the "infant corps."

In Europe of the Middle Ages, many things had changed from the days of the Roman Empire, but officers, or knights, as they were called then, still rode on horseback and they still employed boys to help them to get ready for battle. At this time they had even a greater need for servants, because now they wore heavy suits of armor. It took hours to get into a suit of armor, and hours more to mount a horse once it was on. The armor of the Middle Ages was so heavy that even the strongest knight could hardly mount his horse alone. At least eight boys were needed to help him. Often that was not enough, and the knight had to be lifted onto the horse with a block and tackle or system of pulleys. If he thereafter fell or was knocked off his horse—well, that was the end. Even the horses wore armor. The boys armored the horses and either lifted their knights onto the horses or operated the pulleys. After that, they put on armor themselves. How they all made it even as far as the battlefield, let alone fought any battles remains a mystery. Nevertheless, that is how it was.

The point is, the boys—the *infanteria*—always went to battle on foot. Later *infanteria* was used to mean all of the armored soldiers who clanked and creaked on foot behind the knights on horseback. In English, the word became infantry.

Kidnap

Definition: To kidnap is to capture a person and hold that person prisoner until money is paid for his or her release. The word is a compound of two slang words of Middle English.

Between the seventeenth and eighteenth centuries, while England was establishing colonies in America there was a great demand for cheap labor in the New World. Forests had to be cleared, swamps drained, roads built, and homes and people cared for. Much of this work was done cheaply by slaves and indentured servants. But somehow, there were never enough people to get all the work done, and wealthy landowners and businessmen were constantly looking for help in any way they could get it.

Now in London at this time conditions for the poor were dreadful. Many families had not enough money or food to care for their children, and they turned them out to fend for themselves. Children slept in the streets and stayed alive by begging and stealing. There were many people who saw in this situation a chance to make a quick profit from the wealthy people in America. They would approach these poor homeless children with fantastic tales of a great life in America. Then they would coax them into the filthy holds of cargo ships and take them off to the colonies. If the children were too wise to believe them, and refused to go, they beat them or drugged them and dragged them off anyway.

On arrival to America they would sell whatever children survived the awful conditions on board ship to the colonists.

The practice came to be known as kidnapping. *Kid* was Middle English slang for child, and *nap,* slang for "steal." Kidnapping was "child stealing."

Eventually, social conditions in London improved and homeless children were better protected. Kidnapping was outlawed, and many suspected kidnappers were brought to trial and punished. One confessed that he had transported to America five hundred children a year for twelve years—six thousand children!

Money/Mint/Dollar/Quarter (Two Bits)/Dime/Nickel/Penny/Coin

Definition: Money is pieces of metal and pieces of paper which are exchanged for goods and services. All nations today use a combination of paper and metal coins. In the United States, the paper is dollars, *and the metal is coins called* half dollars, quarters, dimes, nickels *and* pennies. *Everyone knows that, but not everyone knows where they got their names. The names come from Latin, French, German, Dutch, Old English and Middle English.*

Money/Mint

In ancient Rome there was a temple which was called Moneta, in honor of the goddess Juno. The first Roman coins were made of copper. In 269 B.C. silver coins were made at *Moneta,* and were given that name so that everyone would know they were made of silver and not copper. *Moneta* then came to be known not only as a silver coin but also any place money was made.

As the Romance languages were developing out of Latin, and other languages were coming together to form English, *moneta* went through a series of changes until it took the modern form in English as mint. A mint is a place where money is made. Our word money comes from the Latin *monetarius,* which means "having to do with the mint."

Coin

In ancient times designs were hammered or stamped into a piece of metal with a wedge-shaped tool called in Latin a *cuneus.* In Old French this word became *cuigne,* then *coing.* In Middle English, *coing* became *coin.* Soon, coin was used to mean not only the tool itself, but that which it made—a stamped coin.

Dollar/Pieces of Eight/Two Bits, Four Bits, Six Bits

In Czechoslovakia in 1516, there lived a man called the Count of Schlick. He had an estate in the valley, or *thal,* of Joachim. On his estate he minted his own coins. The coins had the face of St. Joachim stamped on them, and came to be known as *Joachimsthalers,* a word which meant "from the valley of Joachim." In Germany and Holland the word was shortened to *thaler,* and then, *daler.* The name came into England as dollar.

Now, the English called their own money pounds, shillings, and pence. They used *dollar* to mean the gold coins of Spain which were circulating in England. Another name the English had for the Spanish gold coins was "pieces of eight." The reason they were called that was that each Spanish gold coin was worth eight English shillings.

When the American colonies won their independence from England, they no longer used English pounds, shillings and pence. They began to mint their own, and they called it *dollars*. A dollar was the same as 100 cents, 20 nickels, 10 dimes, 4 quarters, or 2 half dollars. In slang, then as now, a quarter was two bits, a half dollar four bits, and 75 cents six bits. This is why:

When Americans first minted their dollars there was still much Spanish money circulating in the country. Remember that the Spanish gold coins were called pieces of eight by the English because the coins were the same value as eight English shillings. The Americans decided to make their dollar of equal value to the Spanish pieces of eight. Now, in English slang, a shilling is a *bit*. If there are eight bits in a Spanish coin, there are eight bits in an American dollar, and each bit is worth twelve-and-a-half cents. One eighth of the Spanish coin, or one eighth of the American dollar was equal to one English shilling or bit, or 12½ cents. Two times 12½ equals 25, so 25 cents—or a quarter—came to be known as two bits. It is easy to see why half dollars were called four bits and 75 cents, six bits.

Cent/Penny

Cent comes from the Latin *centum* meaning hundred. Since a dollar can be divided into one hundred coins, each coin would be one one-hundredth of it. For this reason one one-hundredth of a dollar is called a cent.

A cent is also called a penny. This comes from the Old German *pfenning*, which meant any coin. *Pfenning* became *penning* in Old English, and finally penny in the modern language.

124

Nickel

Except for the nickel all the other coins which make up a dollar—half dollars, quarters and dimes—are named for what percentage of the dollar they are worth. A fifty-cent piece is made up of fifty percent, or one half of a dollar and is called a half dollar. Half comes from Old English *healf,* meaning to cut in two. Twenty-five-cent pieces are known as quarters because they are one-fourth of a dollar. Quarter comes from the Latin *quartus,* meaning the number four. Each dime is one tenth of a dollar. Dime comes from the Latin *decima,* meaning ten. This became *disme* in Old French, and *dymes* in Old English. From *dymes* it became the modern English dime.

A nickel is named for the metal it is made of—part copper and part nickel. The original meaning of nickel had nothing to do with either money or metal. In Old German *nickel* meant "demon."

From ancient times clear through the Middle Ages and into the present people have mined different metals. Copper has always been much in demand to make tools, weapons, jewelry and parts of machinery. During the Middle Ages German copper miners kept finding an ore which looked exactly like copper but was not. No matter what they did with it, they could not get copper from it. In disgust, they named this mysterious stuff *kupfernickel,* which meant copper-demon. They believed devils had invaded the mines, stolen the copper and replaced it with worthless junk.

A Swedish mineralogist named Alex Cronstedt did not believe in demons. He began to work with the kupfernickel to see if he could get a metal from it. In 1751 he succeeded, and the metal he extracted from the ore he named *nickel.*

The American five-cent piece, which is one twentieth of a

dollar, could have been named a *twentig,* which is the Old English word meaning two times ten. But it was not, it was named a nickel, after the metal it is made of.

Pen/Pencil/Penicillin

Definitions: A pen can be a writing instrument or a place to fence in animals. Their sources are different. The pen for animals comes from the Middle English penn. *The pen we are talking about here is the writing instrument, and the word comes from Latin. A pencil is a writing instrument which does not use ink. Penicillin is an antibiotic medicine made from mold. Both these words come from Latin, but from a different word than pen.*

From ancient times clear up to the nineteenth century, people wrote with the points of quills, or feathers. The Latin word for feather is *penna.* Shortened to pen in English, the word

was used along with quill to mean a feather used for writing. It is hard to believe that the ballpoint we use today had a feather as its ancestor.

Although both pen and pencil have similar spellings and both are used for writing, pencil comes from a different source. It comes from the Latin *penicullus,* meaning "little tail." Artists called their tiny, fine-pointed brushes *peniculli* because they looked like the tails of little animals. Sometime around the sixteenth century someone became tired of dipping a quill into ink a dozen times just to write one sentence. So he invented the pencil. Because it was made of soft graphite which could be sharpened to a point, and because it could mark a line as fine as that of a paintbrush, it was named after the *penicullus.*

Penicillin comes from a mold. When the mold was put under a microscope, it looked as if it were made up of thousands of tiny tails. Like the paintbrush and pencil before it, it was also named after the *penicullus.*

Salary

Definition: Salary is money paid for the work done. It is paid regularly, by the day, by the week, by the month, or by the year. The word comes from Latin.

In the days of the Roman Empire, soldiers marched in all kinds of weather, in every kind of climate. Much of the desert land of the Middle East was part of the Roman Empire, and soldiers spent months at a time on the broiling hot sands. Their bodies could easily have been drained of salt which is essential for good health. Also, the food they carried had to be preserved in salt so that it would not spoil. Finally, they had a keen taste for highly spiced food and seasoned their food with great amounts of salt, just for the pleasure of it.

The Latin word for salt is *sal*. Roman soldiers were paid a regular wage for their work. Then, several times a year, they were paid something extra to satisfy their need and liking for salt. The extra pay was called *salarium,* meaning "money for salt."

By the third century, all connection between *salarium* and salt disappeared, and *salarium* came to be known as any regular pay. The word came into English as salary.

Sirloin

Definition: The sirloin is the part of the cow, or beef, which is just above the loin, the tenderest part. Sirloin is cut up to make roasts and steaks. The word comes from French.

Some say Henry VIII of England first coined the word sirloin. Others say it was either James I or Charles II. In any case, one of these kings was supposed to have been so delighted with a delicious, tender piece of beef that he decided to make it a knight. Knights are addressed as "Sir."

According to the story, the king enjoyed the meat and ate heartily. Then, belching with contentment, he startled the whole court by whipping out his sword and swinging it over his head. Seconds later, he laid the sword on what was left of the meat and roared, "I dub thee Sir Loin!"

Like the story of marmalade, this seems to make sense, but it is not true. Sirloin actually comes from the French *surloin. Sur* in French means "above." *Surloin,* then, means "above the loin." Because they probably believed the story, and because the English mispronounced the French, they spelled the word sirloin, and that is the word we use today.

128

Slave/Slav

Definitions: A slave is a human being who is owned by another human being and forced to work for the owner. A Slav is a member of the group of people who first settled in eastern Europe in what is now Russia, Poland, Hungary, Czechoslovakia and Yugoslavia. Both words come from Latin and Old Germanic languages and are related to each other.

The reason these two words, which look so similar, have such different meanings is simply that at one time the Slavs were slaves.

In the sixth century, a people from the area along the Baltic Sea, in the region now called Poland, invaded the land of the Germans. Now usually when one group invades another, the invading group is victorious. In this case, the opposite was true.

The Germans were more warlike than the invaders, and they defeated them. They threw them into prison, forced them to work for them, and sold them to the Greeks and Romans. The Romans called the defeated invaders *sclavus,* and the Germans called them *sclaves.*

From these words came Slav—meaning anyone from the region of the Baltic Sea—and slave, anyone who is bought and sold and forced to work.

Sleuth

Definition: A sleuth is a detective. The word comes from the Norse language of the Vikings.

The early Norsemen were excellent hunters. Like the American Indians, they could read the signs left by a hunted animal and track it down with ease. Their word for the track left by an animal was *sloth.*

129

When the Norsemen invaded Britain, the English quickly learned their hunting practices. In Old English the word for the trail of an animal or person on the run became *sleuth*. Dogs were often used for hunting, and they were even better than humans at tracking. There were many legends of dogs' skill and heroism, as there still are today. Hunters' dogs were called sleuth hounds.

In the late nineteenth century, an American named Allan Pinkerton started an agency to track down escaped criminals and missing persons. Later, the agency expanded to include detectives who hired out to solve any kind of mystery. They were all so good at their jobs they were compared to the hunting dogs of the Norsemen and called sleuths.

Tawdry

Definition: Something tawdry—jewelry, clothing, furniture—is something which looks expensive, but is really a cheap, poor-quality copy. The word comes from a phrase in Middle English.

This story begins way back in the seventh century with an Anglo-Saxon princess named Etheldreda. Etheldreda's father forced her to marry a king she did not love. Being a willful and independent lady, she took her jewels and her waiting women and fled to an island named Ely. She then bought Ely and with her women set up a convent of nuns.

Then, as now, nuns were to give up worldly things, live very simply and devote their lives to God. According to the church, overfondness of worldly things is vanity, and vanity is a deadly sin. Although Etheldreda had become a nun, she could never give up her habit of wearing many gold chains around her neck. Legend tells us she died painfully of a growth in her throat, and some believed the growth was punishment for Etheldreda's vanity of wearing gold chains. This was her only sin, it seems. In every other way she must have been an excellent nun and truly a holy woman, because, after her death, the church made her a saint.

By Chaucer's time, some seven hundred years later, when the language was Middle English, the name Etheldreda had been changed to Audrey, and the princess was known as St. Audrey. Every year fairs were held around St. Audrey's convent. At those fairs, just as at today's carnivals, pitchmen and peddlars sold cheap, silly little objects and trinkets. In memory of St. Audrey's small sin and great punishment, gold chains were sold by the hundreds. In those days, anything worn around the neck was known as lace, even things made of metal. The laces, or necklaces, sold at the fairs were not St. Audrey's chains, of course, and definitely not gold; they were merely cheap copies. But they were advertised as the real thing. The peddlars would show their wares and cry, "Saint Audrey's lace, Saint Audrey's lace for sale!"

As we have seen in the stories of bedlam and debonair, the English always managed to run phrases and long words together so that the originals would be nearly lost completely. As the pitchmen hawked their wares, "Saint Audrey's lace" sounded something like "Sin't'Audrey's lace" then "sin t'audreys" then "taudreys" and finally, "tawdry." From then on, tawdry was a word used for any cheap copy of a fine and valuable original.

Town/Metropolis/City/Village/ Hamlet

Definitions: A town is a center of government and business. It is usually larger than a village or hamlet, but smaller than a city. The word comes from Old English. Village comes from French. Hamlet comes from German. City comes from Greek. A very large city is known as a metropolis. The word comes from Greek.

All of these words, except town, come from words having to do with government, farms or homes. A very large city is known as a metropolis or metropolitan area. The word comes from two Greek words: *meter* and *polis*, meaning "mother" and "police." In ancient Greece, cities were actually like separate, independent nations and were known as city-states. City comes from Greek and Latin words having to do with citizens, a place of government. The metropolis in ancient Greece was the "mother city," or the largest and chief of the other city-states.

Village comes from the Latin *villa* and the French *ville,* meaning "farm." Early villages were clusters of buildings on the great farming estates of the Middle Ages. There, people made the tools, weapons, furniture and clothing used by the lords of the estates.

Hamlet comes from the Old German word *ham,* meaning "home." A hamlet was a small group of buildings, a little "home" for a small group of people.

Town had nothing to do with government, farming or home. The word comes from an Old English word meaning "hedge." During the Middle Ages in Europe no farmer dared stay all night in his fields. He could be murdered by roving bands of robbers or attacked by wild animals, such as bears, wolves or wild boars. So, at sundown, farmers walked back from their fields to an area of little houses which was surrounded by a hedge to keep out the wild animals. The Old English word for hedge was *tun,* which was pronounced "toon." Later, the hedges were replaced by walls, which were much better protection against robbers and wild animals. But the word remained, meaning at first any collection of buildings surrounded by a wall, and then, a larger center of business and government.

The words metropolis, city, town, village and hamlet, or parts of them, are used in the names of many American metropolitan areas. There is Minnea*polis,* Minnesota and Indiana*polis,* Indiana, for example. There is Atlantic *City,* New Jersey and Oklahoma *City,* Oklahoma. Village appears in Louis*ville,* Kentucky and Nash*ville,* Tennessee, and we see hamlet in Birming*ham,* Alabama and Belling*ham,* Washington.

Town appears in Allen*town,* Pennsylvania and Youngs*town,* Ohio. There are many, many more examples like these. How many can you think of?

133

Urchin

Definition: An urchin is a mischievous child. The word comes from Latin by way of French.

In Latin the word *ericius* means "hedgehog." A hedgehog is a little animal somewhat like a porcupine with stiff, spiky fur. In French, the word became *herichun*. The English struggled with the spelling and pronunciation of that word, making it *hurcheon, irchin* and finally urchin.

In the Middle Ages people believed that the spiky little body of the hedgehog was really a cover for a goblin or trouble-making elf. So, urchin came to mean that particular kind of creature which disguised itself as a hedgehog.

In the story about "kidnap" we saw that many people in the Middle Ages were so poor they could not keep their own children, and they turned them out into the streets to fend for themselves. Those children who did not die grew into grubby, fearless little creatures who lived by their wits. They stole, did various mischief and showed little respect for their elders. Looking at them, people were reminded of those fresh little elves who were supposed to live in the bodies of hedgehogs, and they began to call the children urchins. Mischievous children have been called urchins ever since.

Yankee

Definition: Yankee is the nickname for American. Gringo (see next entry) is a name Latin American people give to North Americans. No one knows exactly where these words come from or when they were first used, but Yankee probably comes from Dutch, and gringo *from Old Spanish.*

It was first thought that Yankee came from a Massachusetts Indian mispronunciation of "English." Another theory is that it came from the name of a Dutch sea captain called Yanky. Still another theory says it comes from the Dutch name Janke. In Dutch *j* is pronounced like *y*, and *-ke* is added to a name to mean "little," just as we turn "Jim" into "Jimmy."

The theory that most linguists agree on is this: In the sixteenth century, Germans nicknamed Dutchmen, whom they didn't like very much, Jan Kaas, meaning "John Cheese." During the days of the buccaneers, English sailors called Dutch pirates Jan Kees. (Remember, the *j* is pronounced like *y*.) The word came to mean any pirate.

In the seventeenth century, before New York was English it belonged to the Dutch, and was called New Amsterdam. While both the English and the Dutch had colonies in the New World, there was much bad feeling between them. The Dutch realized that Jan Kees was an insulting name meaning pirate. So, instead of accepting that name for themselves, they used it to mean Englishmen, who were *all* pirates, as far as the Dutch were concerned. For the next one hundred years dictionaries of English listed *jankee* or *Yankee* as a word for pirate.

In the meantime, settlers in the colonies of Connecticut, Vermont and Massachusetts—the part of the United States known as New England—decided they liked the nickname and used it proudly to indicate their rugged independence and cleverness at defeating the British during the American Revolution. By the eighteenth century, Yankee was accepted as a name for all New Englanders. During the American Revolution the British called all American colonists—northern and southern—Yankees.

During the American Civil War in 1865, southerners called the northerners Yankees. As the United States grew into a large nation and came into contact with the rest of the world, all Americans were known everywhere as Yankees.

135

Gringo

Latin Americans call North Americans Yankees, but they spell the word *yanquis*. Another word they use for North American is *Gringo* (GREEN-go). It is included in American dictionaries. There are two theories for the origin of the word.

One theory says it comes from an old English folk song which begins, "Green grow the lilacs all around, all around . . ." During the war between the United States and Mexico, American soldiers adopted the song as their marching song. According to this theory, the Mexicans heard "green grow" as "green go" and thereafter coined "gringo" as a nickname for Americans.

The other theory says the word originated in the Spanish of Spain, and comes from their word, *griego* which means "Greek." It is said that when the Spanish first heard the language of the Irish, it sounded so strange to them they called it Greek. After that, they called any foreign language Greek. They must have said to themselves, as we often do when we don't understand something, "It's all Greek to me." As the years passed, *griego* was altered to *gringo* and came to be used only for speakers of English, especially Americans.

INDEX

• • •

Abacus, 96-97
African language, 47
Alfred the Great, 23-24
Alice in Wonderland, 55
Alphabet, 45
  Cherokee, 92-94
  Sanskrit, 7
American Indian languages,
    45, 47, 48, 92-94
  words, 49-51
American Revolution, 90
Ampere, André M., 52
Ancestor languages, 7-11
Anglo-Saxon. *See* Old English
Anglo-Saxon Chronicle, The, 24
Applaud, 97-99
Arabic language, 45, 47, 105
Arkansas, 79
Artisan, 74
Art words, 29-30
Asia, British conquest of, 44
Assassin, 61-62

Assassination, 61-62
Athens, 70-71
Australian language, 47

Ballot, 99-100
Balto-Slavic languages, 8-9
Bangs, 77-78
Barbecue, 62-63
Battle of Marathon, 71
Bazooka, 78-79
Becket, Thomas à, 85-86
Bedlam, 83-84
Bellona, 115
Berserk, 100-102
Bethlehem, 83-84
Blackball, 99-100
Blackmail, 102-103
Black Death, 104-105
Bonfire, 103-105
Borrowed words, 41-48, 52,
    61-76
"Bow-wow" theory, 5

Britons, 16-17
Buccaneer, 62, 64-65
Burns, Bob, 78-79

Calculate, 96-97
Calculator, 96
Calculus, 96-97
Canter, 85-86
Canterbury, 85-86
Canterbury Tales, 32, 35, 39, 86
Carroll, Lewis, 55-57
Caxton, William, 37
Celtic language, 8-9, 18
Celts, 16-18, 20-21
Cent, 124
Charles II, King, 128
Chaucer, Geoffrey, 32, 33, 34,
    35, 36, 39, 86, 131
Chauvin, Nicholas, 86-87
Chauvinist, 86-87
Check, 105-108
Checkers, 105-106
Checkmate, 105, 106
Cherokee language, 92-94
Chess, 105-107
Chesterfield, Lord, 52
Chinese language, 41-43, 45,
    47
Chocolate, 45
Churchill, Winston, 58, 113
City, 132-133
Civil War (U.S.), 135
Coconut, 65-66
Coin, 122-123
Congress, 68-70
Copper, 125
Cronstedt, Alex, 125
Crusades, 36, 41, 44, 62, 113

Curfew, 108-109

Daladier, Edouard, 81
Dark Ages, 19, 22-23, 36, 49
Debonair, 109-110
Dime, 122, 124
Dismal, 110-111
Dollar, 122-123
Dragon, 112-113
Dragoon, 112-113
Dumbbell, 66-67
Dutch language, 7, 9, 11, 25,
    26, 46, 62, 66, 68

Eadred, King, 24
Easel, 67-68
East India, British conquest of,
    44
Elizabeth I, Queen, 72
Ellicot, Andrew, 89-90
English language. *See*
    Borrowed words; Middle
    English; Modern English;
    Old English; specific
    words
Etheldreda, 131-132
European colonization, 44, 49
Exchequer, 105, 107
Explode, 97-99

Falcon, 110
Fashion words, 29-30
Fawkes, Guy, 87-88
Filibuster, 68-70
Flemish language, 46
Frankish language, 18, 27
Franks, 18
Frantic, 113-115

French language, 7, 9, 10, 11, 18, 23, 27-32, 35, 45, 46, 52, 66, 73, 74, 108, 109, 110, 128
Friesian language, 46

Germanic languages, 8-11, 18, 23, 52
German language, 7, 9, 10, 23, 46, 66
Gossip, 115-117
Government words, 29
Grammar, 31
Greek language, 7-10, 17, 45, 53-55, 70, 112, 118-119, 132
Gringo, 134, 136
Guy, 87-88

Hamlet, 132-133
Handicap, 117-118
Hashish, 62
Hebrew language, 47
Hellenic language, 8-10
Henry II, King, 32, 85-86
Henry VIII, King, 84, 128
Heresy, 104
Hitler, Adolf, 115
Hobby, 79-80
Hobby horse, 79-80
Horse, 77-78, 120-121

Idiot, 118-119
Imitative words, 53
Immigration, 44
Indian languages, 8, 47
Indo-European languages, 7-11, 12-14, 16

Indo-Iranian languages, 8-9
Infantry, 119-121
Invented words, 52-58, 77-82
Irish language, 7, 9, 46
Italian language, 9, 11, 45, 46
Italic languages, 8-11

Jabberwocky, 56
James I, King, 128
Joachim, 123
Julius Caesar, 37-39

Kidnap, 121-122

Languages
  ancestor, 7-11
  development by century, 44
  families, 12-15
  group comparisons, 12-15
  Middle English, 9, 10, 16, 26, 27-33, 34-35, 121, 131
  Modern English, 5, 9, 10, 12, 16, 21, 25, 33, 34-40
  most spoken, 41
  new words, 44
  Old English, 9, 12, 16, 21, 22-26, 27-32, 40, 52, 103, 115-116
  origin of, 5-6
  pre Old English, 16-21
  See also specific languages
Latin language, 9, 10, 11, 17, 18, 23, 24, 35, 45, 53-55, 96, 97, 99, 110, 113, 119, 123, 124, 126, 127, 134
Law words, 29
Learning words, 29-30
Lombards, 18

Lynch, 89-90
Lynch, Colonel William, 89-90

Marathon, 70-71
Marmalade, 72
Mary, Queen of Scots, 72
Metropolis, 132-133
Mexican Indian language, 47
Mexican War, 44
Middle Ages, 66, 73, 74, 102,
    103, 104, 108, 110, 111,
    120, 125, 133, 134
Middle English, 9, 10, 16, 26,
    27-33, 34-35, 121, 131
Military words, 29-30
Mint, 122-123
Modern English, 5, 9, 10, 12,
    16, 21, 25, 33, 34-40
Moneta, 122-123
Money, 122-123
Montague, John, 90-92
Mother, 13
Mr. Smith Goes to Washington,
    70

Names, 83-95
Napoleon, 87
Nickel, 122, 124
Night, 13
Nonsense words, 55-57
Norman Conquest, 27, 29
Norse language, 9, 10, 100,
    129
Norsemen, 18, 20, 23, 24, 101,
    129-130

Old English, 9, 12, 16, 21,
    22-26, 27-32, 40, 52, 103,
    115-116

Old words, 96-136
Olympic Games, 70-71

Partridge, Eric, 81
Pasteur, Louis, 52
Peasant, 74
Pen, 126-127
Pencil, 126-127
Penicillin, 126-127
Penny, 122, 124
Persia, 70-71
Persian language, 7, 47
Personal names, 83-95
Pheidippides, 70-71
Phony, 81-82
Picts, 16, 17, 20-21
Pinkerton, Allan, 130
Place names, 83-95
Plutarch, 37
Portuguese language, 9, 11, 65
Prefixes, 53-55

Quarter, 122, 124

Raccoon, 50-51
Radish, 45
Religious words, 29
Renaissance, 36-37, 44
Rhythm, 51
Robe, 73
Romance languages, 11, 123
Roman empire, 35, 49, 120,
    127

Sabotage, 74-75
St. Audrey. *See* Etheldreda
St. George, 113
Salary, 127-128

Sandwich, 90-92
Sandwich, Earl of. *See* Montague, John
Sanskrit, 7-9, 75
Schlick, Count of, 123
Scots, 16, 17, 20-21
Scottish language, 9, 46
Sequoia, 92-95
Seven, 13
Shakespeare, William, 36-39
Sirloin, 128
Slav, 129
Slave, 129
Slavery, 44
Slavic languages, 9, 46
Sleuth, 129-131
South African language, 46
South Pacific languages, 47
Spanish language, 9, 11, 43, 46
Speech, origin of, 5-6
Spooner, William A., 95
Spoonerism, 95
Stone Age, 16-17
Suffixes, 53-55
Sulla, 115

Tawdry, 131-132
Tell Them They Lied, 93
Through the Looking Glass, 55, 57
Thug, 75-76
Tomahawk, 51
Town, 132-133

Urchin, 134

Vikings, 19, 24-25, 27, 100-101, 113, 129

Village, 132-133
Volta, Alessandro, 52

Watt, James, 52
Welsh language, 9, 46
West Indian languages, 47
Westward movement (U.S.), 44
Witchcraft, 104, 114-115
Words
    American Indian, 49-51
    art and learning, 29-30
    borrowed, 41-48, 52, 61-76
    fashion, 29-30
    government, 29
    grammar, 31
    imitative, 53
    invented, 52-58, 77-82
    law, 29
    military, 29-30
    nonsense, 55-57
    number in English, 52
    old, 96-136
    religious, 29
    spoken, 6
    written, 6
World War I, 44
World War II, 44, 79, 81, 115

Yankee, 134-135

About the Author
● ● ●

Christina Ashton grew up in Washington State and has spent most of her life on the West Coast, except for about fifteen years, when she lived in Central and South America. She attended Washington State University and the University of Oregon and received a Master's Degree from Dominican College of San Rafael, California.

Mrs. Ashton has always been fascinated by foreign languages, not for their differences, but for their similarities to English. She studied Spanish and French in college and in Central America gained some fluency in conversational Spanish. In Suriname, where she and her husband lived for three years, she learned to understand some Dutch. Although Dutch is the official language of that country, the unwritten dialect of the people is Taki-Taki, a mixture of Dutch, English, Spanish, Portugese, Amerindian dialects and African languages. Mrs. Ashton made a study of Taki-Taki and compiled her findings into an English/Taki-Taki dictionary.

After many years of teaching English to foreign students, she decided to put her fascination with English word origins into this book.

Currently, Mrs. Ashton lives in San Mateo, California, where she works as a teacher and free lance writer.